NONNI IN JAPAN

Around the World at 80 Years Old!

by

Jon Svensson

Translated by

Friederika Priemer & Aimee O'Connell

Nonni in Japan

English Translation Derivative

Copyright © 2022

Chaos To Order Publishing

All Rights Reserved

ISBN-13: 978-0-9907231-7-2

DEDICATION

We dedicate this work to one of our great "Nonni friends" Konrad Heuvers. Konrad was instrumental in the publication of our first Nonni book "Lost in the Fjord" as he both translated it from the German and provided invaluable guidance and support in its publication. This included pointing out that the story takes place not in the Arctic Ocean but, rather, in the Eyjafjörður Fjord.

Such was the generosity and precision of Konrad. A world-renowned mathematician who published over 25 books and papers and had a long and fruitful teaching career. Konrad also had, in a literal sense, a special relationship with this current work as the "Director Heuvers" of this book is, in fact, his uncle.

John C. Wilhelmsson

CONTENTS

1) Boarding The Steamer "Chichibu Maru" — 3
2) An Educated and Amiable Australian — 7
3) First Impressions of the "Chichibu Maru" — 11
4) A Japanese Boy on Board — 15
5) The Grand Departure for Japan — 21
6) A Japanese Boy Tells of The Hawaiian Islands — 27
7) I Get Acquainted with A Chinese Man — 35
8) The First Night at Sea — 43
9) German Acrobats Successful Performance — 49
10) More Acquaintance with The Acrobats — 57
11) Black Albatrosses Over the Pacific Ocean — 63
12) Under The Supervision of American Warships — 71
13) An Interesting Car Ride Across the Island — 79
14) Leaving Hawaii and Continuing our Voyage — 87
15) Matters Of Life on Board and A Brain Surgery — 99
16) The Soul of the "Chichibu Maru" — 105
17) My Little Friend Speaks of Japan — 111
18) A Farewell Meal with Japan in Sight — 117
19) Seeing An Imperial Japanese Prince — 125
20) Landing In Japan While Thinking of Home — 135
21) How I Was Received in Japan - Arrival in Tokyo — 143
22) My First Impressions of Tokyo — 155
23) Welcomed At Jochi Daigaku University — 163
24) My First Day at Jochi Daigaku University — 171
25) What The Japanese Newspaper Man Told Me — 179
26) I Am Invited to A Japanese Theater — 189
27) I Am Guided to The Japanese Theater — 197
28) I Play a Role on Stage in The Japanese Theater — 203
29) The Acupuncturist with Golden Needles — 213
30) In The Residential Area of Japanese Youth — 225
31) Unexpected Event in The Imperial University — 237
32) I Give a Lecture At "L'étoile Du Matin" — 247
33) More Lectures to Japanese Youth — 259
34) Visit To and Lecture at Mrs. Hani's Giyu School — 275
35) I Am Forced to Give A "Japanese Lecture" — 283
36) A Japanese Hans Christian Andersen — 289
37) A Short Radio Speech to All Children in Japan — 297
38) Speaking To Children in A Japanese Theater — 303
39) In The Palace of The Japanese Emperor — 311
    *Addendum Section — 327

Chaos To Order Publishing
San Jose, CA
www.c2op.com

Nonni in Japan

Nonni in Japan

CHAPTER ONE
Boarding the Japanese Steamer "Chichibu Maru"

Dear Reader,
I invite you to join me here, at the harbor in San Francisco, as I am awaiting the boarding call for the large Japanese steam ship "Chichibu Maru." You might guess from my luggage and the conversation you overhear with my companions that I am about to embark on the first leg of a long and exciting voyage across the Pacific Ocean to completely unknown lands in the Far East. You would be correct, but only in part; for, you see, this is not the beginning of the journey I have been on these past several months. I am, in fact, at the halfway point of a trip around the globe! Having grown up in Iceland, and gone on to study in France and then live in Denmark and other parts of Europe, I have spent nearly seventy years dreaming of seeing the cities and people across the wide Atlantic and Pacific oceans. It was only through the grace of

Nonni in Japan

God and the help of some generous benefactors that I was offered this chance to tour the globe at the age of eighty. And so, the first leg of my journey took me from Europe to North America, where I have crossed the vast continent starting in New York, crossing into Canada and coming into California, where I have enjoyed several weeks but now must prepare for the rest of the journey. It is here where you are joining me as I tell the tale of the second half of my trip around the world!

And so, I approached the huge Japanese ship lying close to the shore of the Pacific Ocean, the great Still Sea. A porter came rushing up, grabbed my luggage and carried it up to the ship. I lingered with the dear people who had accompanied me to the ship, bidding a fond farewell before parting. They would return to San Francisco after I ascended from the shore up onto the ship. Boarding was a slow process, as the deck was fully occupied by people talking noisily to each other. I mused to myself that the

Nonni in Japan

crowd reminded me of an excited anthill. I watched the hustle for a few moments from the ship's railing. My porter, however, asked me to follow him further in, which I did. We descended a few steps onto the deck.
I had hardly gone a few steps when a young Japanese officer approached me with a letter in his hand. He greeted me politely and said: "I do not need to ask your name: You are Nonni, and you are going to Japan." It seems the writer of the letter had described me so perfectly that the officer recognized me at once! He continued: "Our Postal clerk asked me to hand you this letter as soon as you would be on board." He accompanied me down another flight of stairs until we reached my cabin, where he made a polite bow and disappeared.
I read the letter as soon as I entered my cabin. With delight, I saw it was from my Japanese friends in San Francisco, wishing me a happy voyage! I could think of no better way to begin this next stage of my journey.

Nonni in Japan

CHAPTER TWO
An Educated and Amiable Australian

While sitting and pondering the blessing of meeting so many friendly people, the door of my cabin opened gently and a tall young clergyman entered, introducing himself and greeting me in English.

"I am from European descent," said the young clergyman, "but was born in Australia. I am going to China, where I will work as a missionary."

Now I introduced myself: "My name is Jón Svensson." I said, "I am from Iceland, and I am travelling to Japan."

"From Iceland!" exclaimed the young Australian. "You are the first Icelander I have seen in my life! You have surely come a long way!"

He may have felt an Icelander was an extremely rare person, but I reminded him,

"It is an equally rare occasion for me to meet an Australian."

"Well, that is understandable," said the young gentleman. "Our home countries represent completely different worlds."

Only now did I notice that the cabin had two beds, one above the other.

The cabin is probably meant for the two of us, I thought to myself. I asked my visitor: "Have you been assigned a cabin?"

The young Australian replied, smiling: "It seems we are roommates, as this cabin has also been assigned to me."

"That should work well!" I said.

"Yes," answered the young Australian. "And I hope that we will get along well together. After all," he added, smiling, "we have to tolerate each other in this narrow room for over two weeks."

Nonni in Japan

"Tolerate each other!" I laughed. "We shall easily manage. We are almost made to be roommates, even if we do come from lands so far apart."

"Yes, you are right." said the young Australian. "Our homelands may be worlds apart, but we understand each other as if we were compatriots. The sun has burned us only a little differently…"

He wanted to continue, but a young Japanese man appeared in the doorway, pointed to the two beds, and said a few words. Then, he disappeared hastily.

"What did he say?" I asked my new friend.

"He only wanted to affirm that this cabin is meant for both of us."

We chatted a little while longer about this and that. But since we both had some small errands to run, we finally parted with a happy "See you in a bit!" and each went our own way.

CHAPTER THREE
First Impressions of the "Chichibu Maru"

Although I called this "errands," it is more truthful to say I wanted to collect my impressions of the ship. I had the urge to see what was happening out on deck, so that is where I went.

I watched with curiosity and interest the lively hustle and bustle. The deck of the steamer was crowded with people as restless as an excited swarm of bees. The crowd was quite diverse: Europeans, Chinese, Japanese, Mexicans, North and South Americans… all skin tones, all mingling together. One really felt at the crossroads of the world. Nowhere have I noticed the colorfulness of our earth as much as in this place! I felt tremendous joy in this colorful surrounding, and I thanked God for creating something so beautiful.

Nonni in Japan

While completely absorbed in the sight of this picture, I was startled by the ship's whistle, which roared like a thousand furious bulls at the top of their lungs! That startling blast was the first signal for departure.

The crowd's excitement reached its peak, and the groups began to disperse. Mighty masses of people rolled back over the piers and onto the shore. Only the passengers and the ship's crew remained on the steamer. The steam whistle roared again until it was hoarse and began to sound hollow and muffled. Then, things grew more silent. The passengers leaned against the ship's railing opposite the shore and shouted parting words to their relatives and friends down there. The passengers onboard ship towered high above the water.

Unexpectedly, a burst of countless rays of color shot up, out and down from the ship toward the people below. They were cascades of colorful ribbons, and I noticed

Nonni in Japan

there were young boys on board offering them to passengers for a few cents. These streamers were so long that they reached down from the ship's deck to the shore. Passengers would hold one end, throw the streamer, and let the well-wishers on shore catch them as the ribbons rolled back up. By and by, hundreds of streamers hung from the deck to the shore, giving the illusion they might be holding the ship in the harbor. I found this custom most beautiful. I also saw how meaningful it was to the travelers, and how difficult it is for people of all countries to say "Goodbye!"

Nonni in Japan

CHAPTER FOUR
A Japanese Boy on Board

As I stood on deck of the "Chichibu Maru," I noticed a Japanese boy who might have been 12 years old, completely dressed in white and holding a beautiful, rolled-up ribbon in his hand.

When he saw me, he approached, and – to my great surprise – asked in excellent English, "Sir, will you please permit me to give you a ribbon as a gift?"

"That is very kind of you," I replied. "Is this ribbon really your own?"

"Yes, Sir, I have just bought it. It cost two cents."

"Then, my dear little friend, let me give you two cents for it."

"No, no," he insisted. "I want to give it to you!"

Nonni in Japan

"You really want to give me your ribbon as a gift?" I asked, surprised.

"Yes, Sir! Please, won't you take it?"

Amazed, I submitted to his request, even as he was a complete stranger. I was very touched by his childlike friendliness as he handed me his gift. It was indeed a beautiful purple ribbon. After admiring it, I shook his hand and thanked him heartily for his generosity. I said to him: "We both should go to the ship side, to see to whom we should throw this ribbon."

We went to the railing to survey the great crowd of people standing below, waiting for the departure of the ship.

"Do you know anybody down there?" I asked the little boy,

"Yes, I do," he answered pointing to a group of people standing together close to the ship. "These are my friends and relatives," he explained.

Nonni in Japan

"Ah, then," I said, "we will throw the beautiful streamer to them, and nobody else."

By some calls and signs, I tried to catch their attention, soon succeeding.

I said to the boy: "Now, you shout to them in Japanese that we are going to throw them your ribbon."

"No, no, Sir," said the boy, "you must do it alone. Otherwise, they would think the ribbon was mine. You alone must throw them the ribbon because it is yours."

Amazed at the fine character of this boy, I could not refuse his wish. I called a few words in English to the people below as my Japanese friend took a few steps back, in order not to be seen.

"You must not say anything about me!" he whispered.

I obeyed.

Nonni in Japan

I shouted to the people, as loudly as I could, these Japanese words:

"Nippon! Banzai!" (That means something like: "*Japan! Hooray!*" or: "*Long live Japan!*"). At the same time, I threw the ribbon.

"Banzai! Banzai!" answered the people, happily grabbing the beautiful ribbon and holding it tightly. I tied the upper end to the railing.

My young friend continued to hide. It was my farewell, he said, and not his.

Why might he have given me this role? I pondered this a long time, resolving to discover how it is the Japanese instill such impeccable integrity from such a young age.

Nonni in Japan

Nonni in Japan

CHAPTER FIVE
The Grand Departure for Japan

Now, the last farewell signal of the big ship's whistle sounded. Immediately came the roar of machinery from deep within the ship, and our feet felt the tremble and quake as the huge ship was being set in motion. Its work would last somewhat longer than two weeks, with just one short stopover at the Hawaiian Islands, en route from America to Japan.

The mighty ocean giant slowly left the shore.

All those farewell ribbons, which seemed to tie the ship to the land, were torn in an instant. The beautiful steamship "Chichibu Maru" glided calmly and safely out into the deep waters of the vast Pacific Ocean. Our long voyage was underway.

Above on deck, I looked for a solitary place where I could quietly watch the American mainland for the last time; wonderful California would soon dwindle and lie

Nonni in Japan

behind me forever. Right now, we still could see San Francisco, with its many hills and heights, splendid buildings, and wonderful bridges (in my opinion, the greatest bridges in the world!) We moved away from the American continent further and further, and the land and all we could see seemed to sink into the ocean. Most passengers, like me, watched as the shoreline disappeared.

After a few hours, no land could be seen even on the far horizon, only a wide circular line of which our ship was the center. Around us was the nothing but the immensity of the Pacific Ocean. Hour after hour could pass in this infinity without our ever knowing how.

The magnificent "Chichibu Maru," was fully occupied. There were several hundred people on board. Most were Japanese, young and old, including those who had been born in California and had never seen Japan.

Nonni in Japan

I met one Japanese-Californian on the first day of the voyage. He was a young man of about eighteen years, and he greeted me warmly. We chatted for a bit.

"I am guessing that you have been visiting California, and are now going back to your fatherland, Japan?" I asked.

"No, Sir," he replied, "it is my first trip to Japan."

"I had no idea!" I said. "I thought you were Japanese."

"I am Japanese," he answered, "but I was born in California, and have lived there all my life."

"Do you consider yourself true Japanese?" I asked him.

"Yes, I do," replied the young man, "Japan is my fatherland, but California is my country of birth. That's why I prefer to live in California. However, I have a very great

Nonni in Japan

love for Japan, and I am travelling there now, to visit the country of my forefathers."

I caught up with this young Californian Japanese now and again over the course of the voyage, and we talked a bit more each time. He was a very pleasant travel companion.

Nonni in Japan

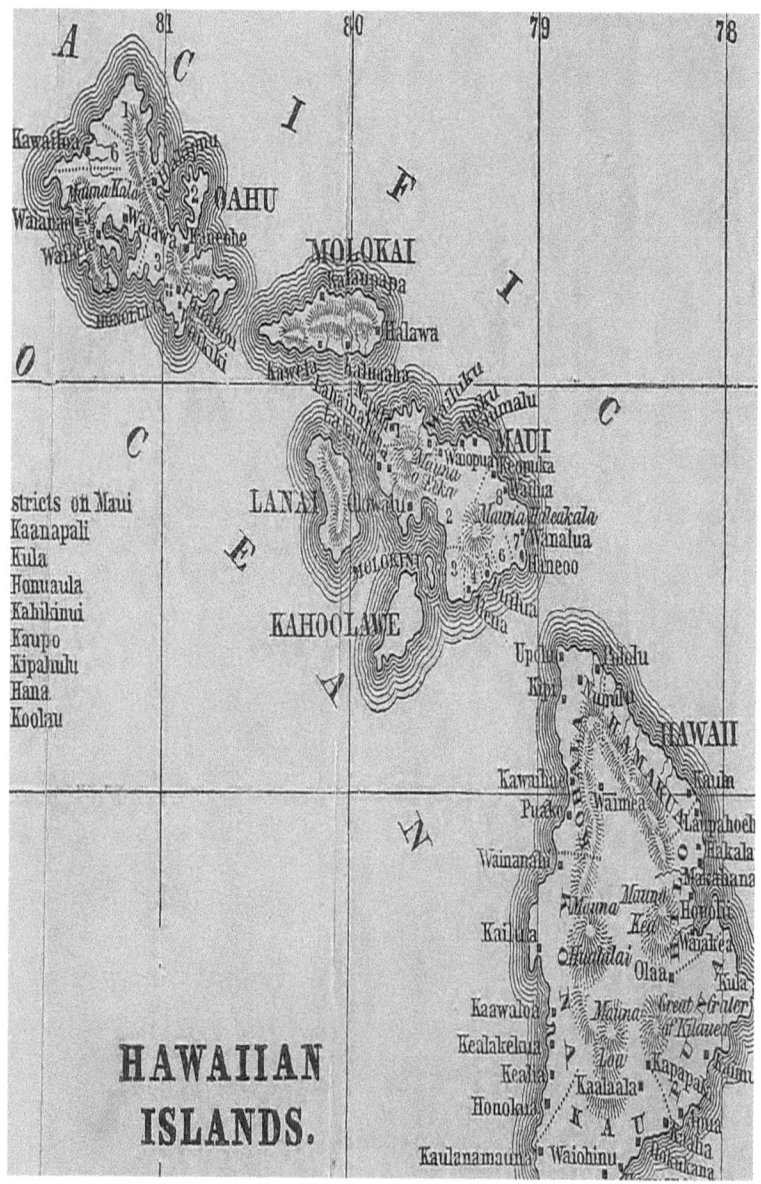

CHAPTER SIX
A Japanese Boy tells of the Hawaiian Islands

I also met up again with the boy who had given me the farewell ribbon at our departure from San Francisco. We became good friends. I continued to marvel at his extraordinarily fine character.

On seeing him the second time, we shook hands, and I thanked him again for his present.

"It was my pleasure," he said.

Feeling a bit tired, I sat down on a small bench, thinking I would abandon myself to my thoughts, feelings, and moods. I said to my young friend: "By now you will want to play a bit with the other boys, won't you?"

"No, Sir!" he said.

"How will you pass the time, then?" I inquired.

Nonni in Japan

The boy looked at me trustingly, and said: "If you don't mind, I would prefer to chat with you a little."

I smiled. "In that case, you are very welcome, my friend!" I pointed to a chair nearby. The dear boy thanked me heartily and sat down beside me. We began a chat that turned out extremely interesting and instructive.

I started him off with a quiz. "A few months ago," I began, "I undertook a voyage from England to the United States of America, across the Atlantic Ocean. Do you think that voyage took as long as the one we are making now?"

Confidently, the boy answered: "Oh, no! The trip across the Atlantic Ocean was much shorter by far."

"Are you absolutely sure?"

Nonni in Japan

"Yes!" he said. As if to demonstrate his point, he asked, "How long did your trip from Europe to America take?"

"It took full five days and nights."

"Only five days and nights! Then, it was not even half as long as our voyage now. It will take us fifteen days and fifteen nights to get to Japan."

I reflected, "In that case, it will take three times as long as the trip from England to America. How do you know this?"

He proudly stated, "I have made this voyage already, when I travelled from Japan to North America."

"Ah! So, you have crossed the Pacific before, and you know how it goes! Tell me then," I continued, "does one experience great storms on the Pacific?"

"No," he said, "the weather is usually calm and quiet, which is why this ocean is called the 'Pacific Ocean,' or just 'Pacific.'"

"Will we pass any countries during this trip, or shall we see nothing but the sky and the water during the whole voyage?" I asked further.

"Only once shall we pass a group of islands," he answered. "For most of the journey, we will be on the ocean without seeing any land."

"What is the name of these islands we shall pass?" I asked him.

"They are called the 'Hawaiian Islands.'"

"Will our ship make a stop-over there?"

"We stop there for half a day, near the capital city of Honolulu. The capital is situated on the island called 'Oahu.'"

"Do many people live on the Hawaiian Islands?" I continued to ask my friend.

"More than two hundred and fifty thousand people live there now, and new people are arriving all the time. I learned at school there will soon be three hundred thousand inhabitants."

"Are there many Japanese?" I further asked.

"Oh yes, there are," he replied. "Almost half of the population is Japanese."

"Do you know the names of all the Hawaiian Islands?"

"I only know the names of five of them," he said, and elaborated: "The five largest islands are Hawaii, Maui, Molokai, Oahu and Kauai." Then he added: "Honolulu is on Oahu, as I said. Our ship will dock at a good harbor, where we will stay for five hours."

"That should give us enough time to have a look at the capital," I remarked.

"Better still," continued the little boy, "we have time to make an excursion by car through the whole island. At the landing site, there is a long row of cars waiting to show travelers around the island."

Nonni in Japan

I was astonished by the clarity and certainty with which the little Japanese boy gave me all these details. I asked him: "My dear boy, how do you know everything so exactly?"

"I have been there myself," he said, "and I also have friends and relatives on the Hawaiian Islands. But, for the time being," continued the little Japanese boy, "we will not see anything but the great Silent Sea for the next several days."

While we were speaking, the signal for dinner was given. The boy shook my hand and said: "Goodbye, Sir. I have to return to my parents."

I pressed his hand, thanking him for all the interesting information he had given me about the Hawaiian Islands, and then I, too, went to the dining room. This meal, called "dinner" by the English, was the last meal of the day. It was already late, and it was already getting dusky.

Nonni in Japan

Nonni in Japan

CHAPTER SEVEN
I Get Acquainted with a Chinese Man

In that moment, passengers came from all sides: ladies and gentlemen, Europeans, Americans, Japanese and Chinese people, and Asian people from different countries of the very far orient. I followed the flow of people. We had to go down a few flights of stairs, then straight on through a long corridor till we entered a magnificent large dining room.

There were many small tables covered with snow-white tablecloths. One had to choose a table and sit down. Since I was completely on my own and did not yet know anyone closely, I did not have a seating preference. Therefore, I did not hurry to choose a table, but remained near the entrance and watched how things developed. The stream of passengers entering was constant, and most of the tables were soon occupied. At last, I decided on a small table near me which was still free.

I had hardly sat down when a friendly looking gentleman in European attire approached me and asked in English: "Excuse me, Sir, are you waiting for a table companion, or are you on your own?"

"I am completely on my own, but I would be pleased if you would like to be my table companion," I said.

"I accept your kind invitation with pleasure," said the unknown gentleman with a smile. Then, he took the empty chair and sat down opposite me.

"I am Chinese," he said, "but have been living in Japan for several years. I enjoy studying different countries and peoples."

"That is a pleasure of mine, too," I said, "and I am travelling to Japan for the first time to get to know its land and people."

Nonni in Japan

The gentleman looked at me questioningly and said: "Do you have a special interest in Japan?"

"Yes," I answered. "I have for many years, even since the earliest days of my youth. In those days I read a lot about Japan. But since coming to America, 'the land of opportunity,' I have met so many Japanese people that my desire to know Japan, 'the land of the rising sun,' has become even greater."

The gentleman's interest grew visibly. "In that case, you have wondered about Japan for a long time," he said, "because, after all, you are not so young anymore."

"You are probably right…" I remarked, and then added, "How many years would you guess I am now?"

The gentleman scrutinized me for a few moments, then said: "I do not dare guess how old you are! But I think it is probable, if not certain, to guess you will soon turn sixty years."

I could not suppress my hearty laughter. "That I will soon turn sixty! I must admit, I feel very flattered!"

"Have I guessed too young?" said the friendly gentleman. "I am sticking to it: you cannot be much older than sixty!"

"As you please, then!" I said, still laughing. "Not much older than sixty!"

"Yes, that's what I think, for sure," replied the gentleman.

I took my passport out of my pocket and handed it over to him, as it showed my exact age. He took the passport and examined it thoroughly. There was the year of my birth: 1857.

Greatly amazed, he looked at me closely. "Am I to believe what is written on your passport? According to this, you are eighty years old! This must be an error!"

"No, Sir," I assured him, "it is no error. I am indeed eighty years old. But I have kept company with young people all my life, and I rarely think about my age."

He shook my hand and said: "Congratulations, from the bottom of my heart! You bear your eighty years with grace and ease!"

Suddenly he stopped. "Ah! Here comes our waiter!"

I turned round and saw a very nicely uniformed Japanese waiter who greeted us politely, and then asked in good English, "Gentlemen, will you be dining at this table?"

"Yes," we both replied.

"Alright!" said the waiter, turning around, then disappearing. A few minutes later, he returned with our first dish. Without saying a word, he put the food on the table and disappeared again.

"Is this your first trip across the Pacific on this ship?" I asked my table companion.

"Yes, indeed, it is my first trip from America to Japan on this ship," he replied. "But, I have made this voyage more than once with other ships."

"Have you had any storms during those journeys?" I further asked.

"Yes, but these storms only occur in certain seasons. During most of my travels, the weather was nice and the ocean calm, like now. Only in autumn and winter do we sometimes find turbulence in the sea."

We continued chatting comfortably as we ate our meal. When we were almost finished, the gentleman got up, went to the window, and looked out into the dark night.

Then he returned and said: "How lovely it is outside!"

Since I was not quite sure if he was joking, I asked him: "Do you like the view in the dark?"

"Yes, Sir, I cannot deny it: I often go out on deck in the dark, all by myself, and abandon myself to my dreams there, I always get into such deep thought that I hardly want to separate from the night. The night has a strong spirit."

"I do believe you," I answered, "because I know such moods and states of mind very well myself. I suggest that both of us should indulge in that after dinner."

The gentleman agreed, and when we finished, we took leave of each other and went up on the deck into the pitch-black night, each in our own direction.

CHAPTER EIGHT
The First Night at Sea

I have to confess I was seized by a sudden, peculiar shiver when I was completely on my own, outside on the endless ocean in that mysterious darkness of the pitch-black night.

I abandoned myself, speechless, to the enchanting solitude. I peered in all directions, hoping to discover a ship or at least a light somewhere. But all looking was in vain. Only the swooshing of the ship cutting through the sea, and the restless crashing of the waves, could be heard. I could fully understand how this put my Chinese friend into such a poetic mood. I, myself, could have composed my own poetry as I stayed out on deck - far longer than I had planned!

After a long, silent time, polyphonic sounds began drifting up from the interior of the ship. I listened attentively, deciding that something extraordinary must be taking place: the sounds of cheerful laughter, music and merriment mingled together in a carnival-like hustle and bustle.

I groped my way downstairs to see what was happening. And behold! I went from darkest night into brightest light – from deepest silence into loud, lively playing, singing, chatting, and dancing. The very young children were tucked away to bed, but the older children ran about merrily in colorful Japanese attire, like little butterflies: a charming sight for the adults.

Everything was completely different down here from up on the deck, that is true, but it was also quite nice. I looked for a chair, and a boy came running over to help. I recognized him as the Japanese boy with whom I talked for quite some time earlier. Under his guidance I soon found a comfortable seat, and he sat alongside.

I asked him what the occasion might be down here.

He answered, "We just want to be together, to see each other and chat a little." Then he said: "I heard that there is a group of very skillful gymnasts, called 'acrobats," on board the ship with us! They come from Europe, and are travelling to Tokyo to showcase their skills there."

"I am glad you mentioned this, because I had not heard that," I answered. "What else do you know about them?"

"They are ten or twelve young men and young women who perform extraordinary athletic feats."

I asked, "Do you know from which European country they come?"

"Unfortunately, I don't remember. I did hear it, but I've forgotten because I do not know the different European countries well enough."

"Do you think any of them are here with us now?" I asked.

The boy got up and looked in all directions. Suddenly, he bent down and whispered into my ear: "I have discovered two of them. They are sitting opposite us, but a bit to the right, in the last few rows. It is a young man and a young woman, and they are talking together."

Through the help of the little boy, I spotted them. Both made a very good impression and looked between twenty and thirty years old. Judging by their looks I could not discern from which European country they came. They were likely not Frenchmen, Italians, or Spaniards, nor Englishmen. More likely, they were German, Swiss or Scandinavian. However, I did not want to ask them directly.

As time went on, people slowly began returning to their cabins. Soon it became

Nonni in Japan

silent on the ship once again. The night had won and took control over everything.

I bade a good night to the splendid Japanese boy and went to my berth.

Nonni in Japan

CHAPTER NINE
German Acrobats Successful Performance

The acrobats were a subject of conversation among many passengers. At the next morning's coffee, more and more people talked about the acrobats en route to Japan, who themselves were sitting together at some of the small tables in the dining hall.

After coffee I went outside on the deck, where I met three of those interesting athletes: two strong young men, and a young woman. All three were at the railing, looking out over the wonderful sea. When I went past, I greeted them with a hearty "*Guten Morgen!*" ("Good morning!").

All three answered in German, and one of the two young men shook my hand kindly. As I wanted to know from which part of Germany they came, I asked them directly.

"We are from Wuppertal," they replied.

"I know Wuppertal well!" I said. "I have given some lectures there. Wuppertal is a nice city," I added. "I even went by the famous Wuppertal suspension railway."

"Did you also like the surrounding area?" one of them asked.

"Yes, certainly. It is well known that Wuppertal and Remscheid belong to one of the most industrious parts of Germany."

Now they were enthralled. "I would never have guessed," said one of the young men, smiling, "that one of the passengers on this Japanese ship would know our homeland so well."

"Are you traveling to Tokyo?" I continued.

"Yes, we have been invited to appear there at the international games."

"I have heard about that," I remarked. "I am guessing you represent the acrobatic arts?"

The young man said, "Yes."

Nonni in Japan

I asked, "How do you stay in shape, on such a long journey?"

"We practice as often as possible," he responded.

I had little luck seeing the German acrobats in action, as I seemed to be occupied during their exercises on board. Even on the day after I had talked with them, they gave a performance on deck, and I was unfortunately again absent during that time - so I did not see anything of their arts. However, the Japanese boys and their companions were there. After the performance, they came to me and told me with great enthusiasm what they had seen.

I will try and tell you in short what I heard. Of course, the boys' report may exaggerate many things, but I will relate the details exactly as they bubbled out from the young narrators. I believe it was the third day of the voyage, and I was writing a few letters in the peace and quiet of my cabin. My young

Nonni in Japan

Japanese friend, together with several other boys, paid me a visit.

"The German acrobats have given a performance!" they said.

"Oh, have they? Where?" I asked.

"On the deck, at the spot which is normally reserved for passengers."

"Was it nice?"

"Yes, it was incredible!"

"Can you tell me about it?"

"Oh, yes, we can!"

"Fine!" I answered. "I shall be silent and listen!"

Now, one of the younger boys claimed he was able to narrate it in detail. However, the older boys felt he was too young and might exaggerate – so, he stepped aside.

"Let us vote on who should narrate the story," one of the older boys suggested.

That was accepted by everybody. The oldest member of the group took out his notebook and jotted down the names of the young spectators whom he considered the most competent. The boy who got most votes was the elected reporter.

When the elected boy began to speak, all the others were silent. His story went like this, more or less:

"Several of us boys were going to play on deck, but we were asked to make way for the German acrobats, who wanted to perform several exercises. So, we fetched a few chairs and sat down with the other people gathered there. Soon, the acrobats appeared and began their exercises. They were a few men and two young ladies.

"At first, we weren't sure what they were up to, moving about, to and fro. All at once, they stopped… and, without seeing how they did it, a few had jumped up lightning-fast on the shoulders of their comrades, and remained there, upright! Then, one acrobat climbed on the shoulders of the ones who already stood above! Thus, they stood there: three men, one atop the other!

"Those highest up on the shoulders of the others hopped down on the floor with the greatest of ease, like sleek cats! All that happened so easily," continued the young narrator, "that we were not able to see how it really happened. There were many spectators applauding. The English and American audience cried many times *'encore!'*.

"The artists did not have to be asked twice, repeating their feat several times. They did it not always do it in the same way. What astounded us most was the ease with which these extremely agile acrobats jumped onto the shoulders of one another, and how safely they remained up there without losing balance. And, they were even able to do that while the acrobats below were in motion!"

Nonni in Japan

While the boy was still narrating, a few passengers stopped to listen to his report. When he had finished, they added various interesting details of their own, all in highest praise of the German artists.

Afterward, I turned to an adult spectator, a Japanese man, who had been present at the performance, and asked him what he thought about the German acrobats.

"I must say," he said, "that I was truly amazed by their proficiency. What the boy told you was not exaggerated at all. When these extraordinary gymnasts perform in Tokyo, I am convinced that they will be a resounding success."

This assessment was particularly promising coming from a Japanese man, as the Japanese are known the whole world over for their great skill in acrobatic arts.

Nonni in Japan

Nonni in Japan

CHAPTER TEN
More Acquaintance with the Acrobats

The next day, early in the morning, I left my cabin and went on deck. The weather was beautiful as always, pleasantly warm with golden sunshine. The magnificent Japanese ship continued rushing onward through the vast Pacific Ocean. The water surface was shiny and clear, like a mirror. I went close to the railing to get a better view.

That wonderful mirror-like ocean surface truly seemed to expand into infinity. By comparison, looking up into the sky, we might see the sun or the moon, or a cloud will appear occasionally, and there are always the stars at night. The eye can always fix on some point or the other and to rest there. Here, however, when looking over the ocean, there are no boundaries, and nothing for the eye to settle upon, and nothing to define the distance. That vastness seems endless, almost like eternity.

Nonni in Japan

While I was lost in thought, a young lady of about 20 years approached me, pointed to an armchair nearby and said – to my great amazement, in perfect German: "Sir, any time you feel tired from standing, feel free to use that chair and have a rest. Consider it available, as your own, as long as you wish, for I have rented it for the entire voyage."

Although I tried to protest, she said: "No, no! You are older and need to rest more than I do." I had to accept her friendly offer. Renting the chair cost just one dollar for the whole voyage.

That was, however, not the only friendly gesture by the German acrobats that morning. Shortly afterwards, another two appeared and gave me a few photos which they had taken of me while I was standing at the railing, unaware of their presence, writing my impressions into my notebook.

I spoke more with the gymnasts. One told me a very touching story, which I will

Nonni in Japan

mention here in short. Not long ago, the artists gave a performance in a big European city. During that performance a great accident happened:

When one of the girls high up attempted a dangerous jump to one of the heavy ropes hanging nearby, the rope suddenly broke. The unfortunate girl fell and died instantly. Shortly afterwards, the matter was brought to court. The investigation proved that the company which had produced the rope bore the sole fault for the sad accident. The leader of the group was more concerned with returning the girl's body to her fatherland. He paid for a solemn funeral and afterwards had a beautiful monument erected on the tomb. He paid for those costs out of his own pockets.

I talked with the German acrobats for a long while and heard many more interesting stories of their nomadic lives. They had indeed been invited to perform at the

Nonni in Japan

international games; however, the games had been cancelled due to the war with China. I never heard what happened to the acrobats after our voyage.

When I parted with the acrobats, the little Japanese boy, of whom I have told you already several times, appeared again. He greeted me kindly and asked me if he could stay with me for a while.

"With pleasure, my dear little friend!" I answered. "You have already told me so many beautiful things. I would be pleased if you would tell me more!"

Nonni in Japan

Nonni in Japan

CHAPTER 11
Black Albatrosses over the Pacific Ocean

While I sat with the Japanese boy, a flock of pitch-black birds flew over us.

"Do you know what sort of birds they are?" I asked the boy. "I have never seen such birds in my life."

"I know these birds very well," said the boy. "They are albatrosses."

"Albatrosses?" I asked.

The Japanese boy was astonished that I had never seen albatrosses before. He seemed to be quite familiar with them.

As I took a closer look at these peculiar birds, the boy asked me: "What kind of birds follow the ships in Europe, then?"

"The ships on the seas in Europe are followed by seagulls. They are snow-white, not pitch-black, and seagulls are a little smaller than albatrosses."

"Don't be fooled," said my young friend. "Albatrosses are not so large! It is their wings that make them look so big and mighty."

Suddenly the boy put his hand into his pocket and fetched out a small piece of bread.

"Take that bread," he said, "and show it to one of them flying up there. You will be amazed how sharp their eyes are. The albatross will notice it immediately."

I put the piece of bread in my right hand and showed it to one of the birds hovering vertically above our heads. The albatross noticed it immediately and quickly flew down a bit nearer to us. There he hovered on his incredibly large wings, looking at us expectantly. Immediately I threw the piece of bread up to him. In a flash, the nimble bird grabbed it in his beak and flew with it toward the sea, where he dipped it into the water so that he could swallow it better.

Nonni in Japan

When he finished, he flew amazingly fast up to the top of the mast, where he seemed to look down at us gratefully. I observed him just as attentively as he watched us!

I could see that its body was not much bigger than that of a seagull, but the wingspan seemed enormous. He moved his long wings slowly and – it seemed to me – without much effort. He gained speed rapidly, almost as though he could keep pace with our ship as it sailed at full speed. All the other albatrosses flew in the same manner.

When one of the Japanese commanders went past us, I turned to him in English and asked him: "I beg your pardon, Sir. Do you know what wingspan of an albatross might be?"

The commander answered politely: "It is about twelve feet across." Then he nodded to me kindly and walked away.

Both the Japanese boy and I regarded the flock overhead silently for a bit. The boy asked at last, "Can it really be true that their wings are twelve feet across?" I pondered that myself. That would mean each wing is six feet long! Could that be an exaggeration? We observed these most interesting birds for a while still. They needed only to move their wings just a bit more vigorously to shoot forward with incredible speed.

"The albatrosses are skilled aviators," remarked the Japanese boy.

As we stood there, another Japanese commander appeared. I greeted him and asked him in English: "Excuse me, Sir. The albatrosses up there seem to follow our ship the whole day. How can they endure such an exhausting flight for many days?"

He replied: "The albatrosses are among the best fliers of any seabird. They can fly as fast as our ship, even faster, the whole day, without difficulty and without the need to rest."

"How is that possible?" I asked.

The commander smiled and answered: "That is their nature."

"But, what do they do during the night?" I asked further.

The commander replied: "During the night they sit somewhere on top of the masts up there, or wherever they will find a place to rest. Some albatrosses sit on the water and sleep there. They don't need any land. They always live on the water. The only time an albatross seeks land is to lay eggs, most likely on some island. Mother albatrosses will lay eggs in the sand and then stay until they hatch… sometimes even sacrificing their lives, rather than leaving their eggs. As soon as the youngsters are old enough to care for themselves, they live out on the water, like their parents."

Nonni in Japan

I thanked the friendly Japanese commander, and he walked on. My young friend and I were enthralled by these magnificent seabirds. What was the secret of their nature, as the first man had called it? Perhaps his answer was hidden in the smile on his face as he spoke with us. My friend and I mused some more.

"Well… the bigger the ocean, and the longer the birds have to be in the air, I think the longer have to be the wings – as is the case with airplanes," offered my little Japanese friend, to my surprise.

"I like that comparison," I answered, approvingly. "And, then we can say that albatrosses have big wings according to their nature, whereas seagulls have smaller wings, because they do not have to travel so far. Praise the Lord, Who has created everything so wonderfully suited to every creature!"

Nonni in Japan

Nonni in Japan

Nonni in Japan

CHAPTER 12
Under the Supervision of American Warships

Six days and six nights had now passed on the Pacific Ocean aboard the "Chichibu Maru" (flanked, of course, by our mighty albatross companions). The Japanese crew made sure the passengers did not get bored; every day, something different was planned. One day, the captain gave a great first-class lunch. The dining room was decorated with innumerable flowers, and exquisite Japanese dishes were served, accompanied by the most beautiful Japanese music played during the meal. There were also daily cinema shows. Japanese fencing and other sporting exhibitions were offered as well.

Finally, on the sixth day of travel, we were informed that we would enter the harbor of Honolulu, the capital of the Hawaiian Islands, the following day at 10am. We would be granted seven hours to explore the islands. This was greeted with much

Nonni in Japan

anticipation by most passengers, who planned on making excursions of four to five hours by car.

A few American gentlemen invited me to join them on such a trip across the island. I was pleased to accept.

One of the Japanese gentlemen, who had made this trip several times already, told me the following: "America occupies all these islands, and has a military base there."

"There is military on the island?" I asked.

"Yes, Sir," said the Japanese man, "and so, every time a foreign ship arrives, including our 'Chichibu Maru', it will be surrounded by American warships so that nobody leaves the ship without being noticed. The Americans remain nearby and will even accompany us on departure till we have cleared the islands by several miles."

Nonni in Japan

Highly astonished, I replied: "Our visit to the Hawaiian Islands is taken very seriously."

"Yes, extremely seriously," said the Japanese gentleman.

Our visit on the islands sounded like a dramatic affair. I could not imagine how it would all develop, but I found it all rather interesting. I sought out one of the American gentlemen who had invited me to join their excursion group. He was a wealthy merchant from New York. I met him on deck.

I explained, "I have spent several months in the United States of America before travelling to Japan, but I belong to the Scandinavian people, born in Iceland. Here, everything seems unfamiliar to me. I was told that a great part of the people living on the Hawaiian Islands are Japanese, but that the United States occupies the islands. Furthermore, I was told that American warships monitor these islands very closely. Why is this?"

The American gentleman answered patiently, "Americans and Japanese are on good terms. But in the Pacific Ocean, between Japan and North America, there are various islands – for instance, the Hawaiian Islands – which are strategically important for America to occupy. To secure their claim, even the incoming Japanese ships are watched very closely. That is the reason why the American warships are there."

I thought his explanation was clear, and thanked him. We continued to talk for a little while, until he said, "I beg your pardon, but somebody is waiting for me downstairs."

He had hardly disappeared when the Japanese boy came to me.

"May I stand with you?" he asked, as always. "Soon, we shall see the Hawaiian Islands!"

Nonni in Japan

"You are always welcome," I answered. "Have you planned to go ashore?"

"Actually, I did not intend to," he answered. "But, if I may accompany you, I shall go with pleasure."

"I would like that too," I said, "but only if your parents give you permission."

No sooner had he heard that than he rushed to his parents, and soon returned, beaming with joy and their permission. We sat down on a bench up on deck, chatting about this and that, until the Japanese boy jumped up. "There they are! There they are!" he repeated, pointing ahead.

I got up and saw in the far distance a few hills rising – as it seemed – in that very moment.

"That is the highest peak of a mountain near Honolulu," explained the boy.

Nonni in Japan

Both of us watched the interesting landscape become clearer and clearer. The "hill" which I had seen first rose higher by the minute.

Shortly, the boy pointed out: "Those there are not mountains, they are the three warships which will escort us in to port!"

I soon noticed the big ships moving on the horizon. They approached us quickly, and when they were near enough, they accompanied us in the following order: one was on our right side, the other one on the left, and the third one behind us. They remained like that all the way to the harbor of Honolulu.

When the "Chichibu Maru" finally settled into the harbor of the capital, it was 10am.

Both the city and surrounding countryside looked lovely. The island is mountainous, very volcanic and - as it seemed to me – very fertile.

Nonni in Japan

The American gentlemen were soon ready to go ashore. We gathered about each other, and they welcomed my young Japanese friend with pleasure.

Nonni in Japan

CHAPTER 13
An Interesting Car Ride Across the Island

When the landing bridge was moored, we left the ship and entered the city of Honolulu. In total, we were five persons: four adults, and the Japanese boy.

Most people whom we encountered were Japanese. We asked a passerby: "Do you know how many Japanese live in Honolulu?"

He replied, "I don't know about this city, but on the Hawaiian Islands all together, there are approximately one hundred and fifty thousand Japanese people. There are several thousand here in the city, at least."

"How many inhabitants live on the islands all together?"

"Between four- and five hundred thousand," was his answer, and we thanked him for the information.

Nonni in Japan

As we took our first stroll through the city, the most beautiful building we saw was called the old "Royal Palace." We guessed there must have once been a king who was now deposed. None of us knew for sure. While discussing the matter we met another citizen, and we asked our question to him.

"We have not had a king since the year 1893," he answered.

We concluded from this that the isles became a republic at that time.

Walking on, we found a big church in the middle of the city. Nearby stood a big Catholic college. We stopped for a few moments to have a look.

"Can it be that the population here are Roman Catholics?" asked one of the American gentlemen.

"One cannot say so yet," answered one of the other gentlemen, "but a good number of

Nonni in Japan

Roman Catholic Christians lives here. And they are rather active, I heard."

The Japanese boy who accompanied our group asked me in a low voice, "When shall we finally begin the car ride through the island?"

"I think it will be very soon," I answered, "because we are now returning to the beach, where we will find the station at which the cars pick up tourists to drive across the island."

Our walking tour took us back toward the shore, where we noticed an enormous and very modern house. We all stopped and had a look.

"What sort of place is this?" asked one of the gentlemen.

"It is a new hotel which was built recently," answered another gentleman.

"Perhaps we might have lunch there after returning from our sightseeing tour," our

Nonni in Japan

guide suggested, and everyone agreed. Then, we walked on past the beautiful seaside hotel, toward the station on beach. A brand-new car rolled up to where we were. The chauffeur, a Japanese man, got out and politely offered his services.

We arranged that he should drive us through the most scenic parts of the island for about three hours. He would drive us over the mountains which we saw in front of us, and then through an idyllic and fertile valley back to the city. We would be dropped off at the entrance of the hotel so we could then have our lunch.

That was our plan for the afternoon, and it was carried out punctually. We got into the car and departed immediately.

Our chauffeur drove fast across the beautiful, verdant island, stopping occasionally to show us points and items of interest. There were numerous, highly interesting plants and plantations along our

Nonni in Japan

route, including sugar cane, bananas, and pineapples, which grew in such abundance that the inhabitants of the island would find them too many! We asked our guide, "What becomes of such a bounty of fruit and sugar cane?"

"We export them to innumerable countries, all over the world," he replied.

"These islands must be very rich then!" remarked the intelligent little Japanese boy.

"You are right," answered our guide. "In Hawaii, there are many wealthy merchants, and very few poor people."

The country was very mountainous. We drove up hills and then down into fertile valleys, where we saw many farms with people working the plantations. We also drove past beautiful villas and mansions. Our three-hour excursion seemed to go quickly, and we found ourselves back at the magnificent beach hotel once again. We paid our chauffeur and thanked him as we exited the car and entered the hotel's dining room. We chose a table offering a clear view towards the beach and sat down to lunch together.

Everything was as modern as the most noble European hotels. The side of the big dining room facing the sea was one continuous window view to the beach, which we enjoyed watching as we ate. The beach was extraordinarily beautiful, with gentle slopes of fine, white sand leading to the sea. High waves calmly approached and rolled up the broad beachfront, disappearing just before reaching the hotel.

We noticed a great number of people out there enjoying the sea. As I looked more closely, I saw something completely new to me. The American gentlemen and the Japanese boy knew what I was watching, but I had never beheld anything like this.

As the waves rolled up to the beach, I noticed there were "wave riders" gliding in atop them! And, just as strangely, I saw other "riders" gliding from the shore out into the open sea.

Looking closer I noticed that these people carried a long raft when wading from the shore to the water, which they then used like a saddle to sit atop the waves as they rolled through… thus, they "rode" them out to high sea, and were then carried back to shore by the next mighty wave that approached. It was quite entertaining to watch these wave riders while we had lunch!

Nonni in Japan

CHAPTER 14
Leaving Hawaii and Continuing Our Voyage

When we had finished lunch, we left the magnificent beach hotel and returned to our "Chichibu Maru," which was waiting for us patiently in the harbor of Honolulu.

As soon as everybody returned on board, the beautiful Japanese ship was unmoored and allowed to slowly leave the harbor. We had barely begun to move when a great roar made everyone flinch. The American warships which had accompanied us up to the islands were set to escort us off to sea, and from behind a hill on the land there erupted a squadron of monstrous machinery.

"Good Lord! What is that?" cried a few startled ladies near me.

"They are American war planes!" replied a gentleman.

Nonni in Japan

The planes flew in a mad rush over our ship with incredible noise as the warships took up their position. They surrounded us as before: one at the left, another one at the right, and a third ship ahead of us. We were carefully flanked as we entered the open sea, but before too long, we were back on our course to Japan, as fast as the ships could manage.

It was already evening. Soon it became dark, and the lights on the ship were switched on. The lights of the American ships accompanying us shone through the darkness of the night, for several hours. We were far away from the Hawaiian Islands by the time they parted ways with us.

Most of the passengers would likely never see these beautiful, fertile islands again. They will, however, remain in our souls as a lovely and extraordinarily pleasant memory. In front of us was – albeit in far distance still

Nonni in Japan

— the main objective of our journey, that marvelous wonderland Japan.

The next day we were once more surrounded by the Pacific Ocean just as we were when we traveled from San Francisco. I went on deck early in the morning to find a secluded spot in which I might regard the immensely vast water before me.

While I was contemplating the ocean, the Japanese boy appeared.

We greeted each other, and he said: "What an accompaniment the American warships gave us in Honolulu! Apparently, the Americans fear that someone might take away their islands."

"Do you believe that the Japanese ever would?" I asked.

The boy laughed, and said, "We have so many islands ourselves. Japan consists of islands, after all! How should we want to have even more? No, the Japanese do not think of doing such a thing." Luckily, neither of us was much of a politician – one because he was too young, the other one because he was too old.

We left that subject, and I asked my friend, "How long will it take till we reach your fatherland now?"

"It will take a good week," he said.

"Meanwhile, shall we see any other country?" I inquired.

"No," he replied. "We shall see nothing but sky and ocean."

I asked, "If the stretch from the Hawaiian Islands to Japan is equal to the stretch from America to the Hawaiian Islands, does this mean we have half of the journey behind us?"

"Yes, that's correct," said the boy.

Nonni in Japan

I pressed further. "How will we passengers not get bored, if each day passes by exactly like the others?"

"The captain will see to it that we are not bored," said the clever Japanese boy. "Each day he will make sure that the passengers get a variety of entertainment. Thus, he will keep us in great spirits."

"What will he provide for us?" I asked.

"On one of the days, we will have a festive lunch. The tables will be arranged on the higher deck, and everything will be decorated with flowers. And in the evening, when it gets dark, Japanese lanterns will be lit and hung everywhere. There will also be music and all kinds of surprises."

"Have you seen all that?" I asked him.

"Yes," he said, "I experienced that during my voyage from Japan to America."

"In that case, this long voyage will neither be monotonous nor boring," I remarked.

"Certainly not!" continued the boy. "There will still be many other entertainments. For instance, there will be cinema performances, which are quite nice."

"It is amazing," I said, "how much the Japanese do for us travelers."

"Do Europeans not do the same on their ships?" asked my young friend.

"Europeans do a lot," I replied, "but in a completely different way."

I must say that the atmosphere on the "Chichibu Maru" was to my liking. I took my notebook out of my pocket to write down a bit of what was to come.

When the boy saw what I was doing, he said: "Sir, I have often seen you write into that notebook. May I ask what you are writing?"

"It is my pleasure to show you, my dear little friend!" I answered. "I have made a habit of keeping book about my life, because I think it is important to record all the beautiful things which I encounter in the world, so that I can tell other people about it later."

"I like that," said the little Japanese boy.

While we were chatting with each other, the first officer passed by. His name was Matsumura, if I remember. He stopped, greeted us, and asked: "Have you enjoyed the voyage so far?"

"I have enjoyed it very much, thank you," I replied. And, pointing to the Japanese boy I added: "My little friend has also had a good trip thus far."

"I am glad to hear that," he said. "You may expect to enjoy the second part, the voyage from here to Yokohama, because we are not expecting any thunderstorms."

Then he excused himself, as he said the captain was waiting for him at the rudder. He shook hands with us kindly and went towards the front part of the ship.

Nonni in Japan

After he disappeared, I said to the boy: "How polite and friendly that gentleman was!"

"All of them are like that," replied the polite young Japanese boy.

But then I asked, "Did you hear what he said at the end, concerning the navigation of the ship?"

"Sure. He said he had to go to the rudder, at the front of the ship."

"At the front of the ship! Which means to the forward stem! But, the rudder is not found at the front of a ship… it is always at the back of the ship, at the stern post."

"The rudder can also be at the front of the ship," my young friend corrected me. "I have heard this is a recent innovation."

I admit I had not heard such a thing before. I went to the stem to have a look for myself. And, truly! There I saw the peculiar innovation! It looked to be a very complicated mechanism, not easily understood. It appeared as a glass box, with a mysterious mechanism therein, composed of wheels, pins and pointers of shiny metal. The pointers moved on a round disc like the hands of a clock.

The officer on duty noticed my amazement and said to me: "The advantage of this new navigation is that the first mate does not always have to be present."

"Does that really work?" cried the Japanese boy, who had followed me up to the front of the ship.

"Yes, certainly. When the weather is fine and no other ships are nearby, one can leave the ship to itself. By this new mechanism, it can navigate itself alone,"

"That is wonderful!" said the boy, who may have heard about such things, but had never seen for himself until now.

We remained for a while with the friendly helmsman as we all watched the mechanisms working. He made pleasant conversation and had mastered the English language perfectly. When we left, I said: "I am very pleased that I could learn something new from you. However, I feel better knowing that you are at the rudder yourself, and that we passengers are not at the mercy of mere mechanism. I have seen astonishing technical achievements and have great confidence in them, but nothing can ever replace the sight – and especially the heart – of a helmsman!"

"I like that, Dear Sir!" answered the helmsman. "And, you can be assured: I won't rely on the mechanism alone, but will stay at the rudder, allowing the mechanism only to be my assistant."

Nonni in Japan

Nonni in Japan

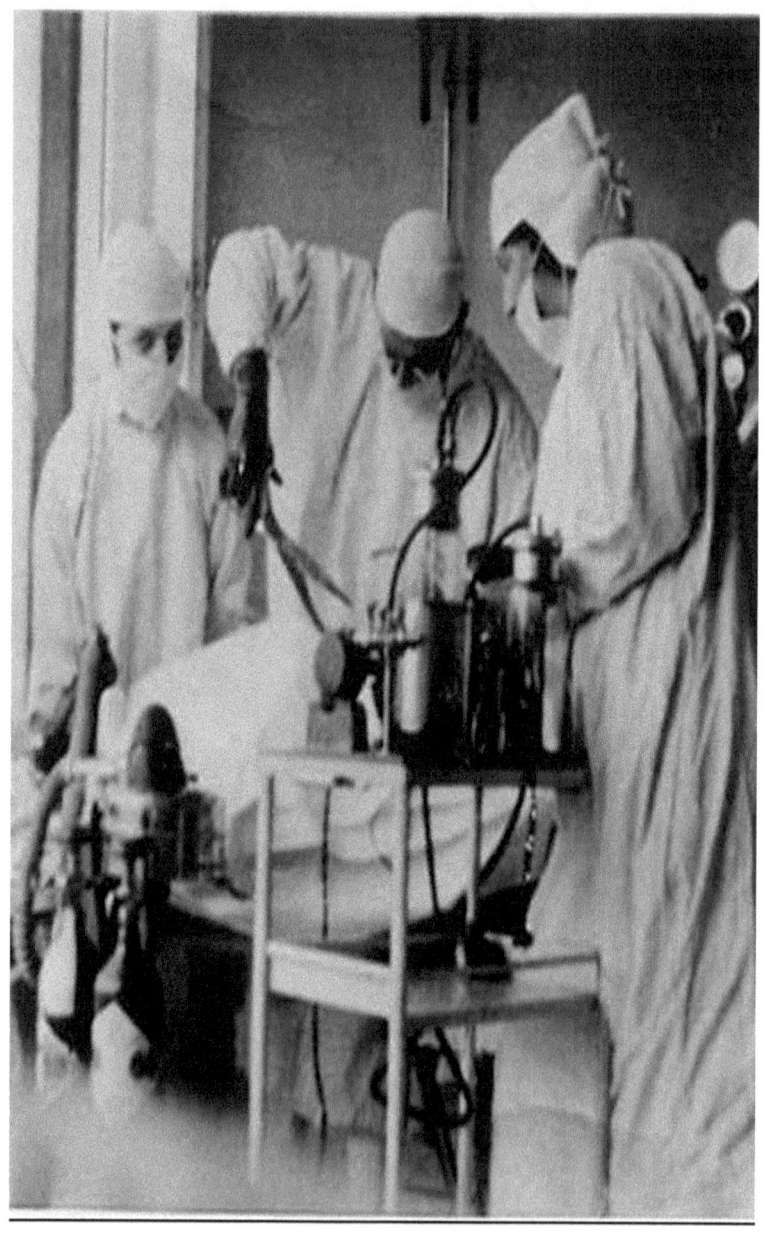

CHAPTER 15
Matters of Life on Board and a Brain Surgery

The little Japanese boy led me downstairs to the lower deck where several passengers had congregated. We fetched two chairs and placed ourselves on a spot where we could take everything in quite well. There, we had another of our familiar little chats.

The boy said: "In which language do you write your books?"

I replied: "Most have been written in German. A few of them I wrote in Danish and French."

"But, you must have written some in English, too," continued the boy, "because I have seen one of your books here on the ship. The title says *'Lost in the Arctic,'* and it is written in English."

"Yes, you are right," I answered him. "However, I wrote that book in Danish. It

Nonni in Japan

was only later translated into English. I have also seen passengers reading it."

"Tomorrow, I shall read it too!" said the boy. "A gentleman who is reading it at the moment has promised to lend it to me when he is finished."

"I am pleased to hear that," I said. "You will not only get to know me better, but also, my brother, Manni, as it is a story about my brother Manni and me. The German title is *'Nonni und Manni'*. Manni was my younger brother."

"Will you ever have your books translated into Japanese?" my friend wondered.

"They will be translated when I get to Tokyo," I said.

"That is wonderful!" he exclaimed. "When all your books are translated in the Japanese language, I shall read them, too!"

As we sat and talked, we were interrupted by the sound of loud music.

Nonni in Japan

The boy jumped up. "I will go have a look at what is going on and come back to tell you."

He went away, then came back shortly to report: "A movie is about to begin in one of the halls nearby."

"Do you know what kind of film it will be?"

"The people said it shows the procedure of a difficult surgical operation."

The others sitting nearby seemed interested to attend. "Film! Film!" was shouted from all directions. Passengers near us got up and went to the auditorium where the movie was to begin shortly. We got up, too, and followed the crowd into the large hall with its stage and many seats. When the auditorium was full, it was darkened, and the presentation began.

In the film, the patient, a young man, was sedated before our eyes. The surgeon stood beside with assistant doctors and nurses to help. The hall was silent as the patient's skull was opened, and with the greatest skill and calm, the surgeon began his work.

To us ignorant spectators, it appeared as if the surgeon was working in the middle of the patient's brain with his knives, pliers and tweezers! The auditorium remained silent as the surgeon continued his precarious and scary work. After approximately one hour, the extremely complex procedure was successfully completed.

During the whole time, the Japanese boy watched in silence. When the performance was over, he turned towards me and said: "A sick patient's life has been saved! I hardly believed such a miracle was possible!"

"You are right," I replied. "It is nothing short of a miracle, a human miracle, which can only be worked by extreme love for sick people and by profound knowledge of the human body."

"Yes," answered the boy. "I could tell by how serious the doctors were. I have never seen anyone working with such dedication. But then, a person's life was at stake, after all."

We stayed together for a while still talking about what we had seen. The little boy could hardly get over it. However, it was getting late, and I asked my little friend if he was feeling sleepy.

"It is past my bedtime," he answered, "but I don't feel tired." I could well understand after what we just witnessed. However, we made our way back to the deck, chatting a short while more in the warm, tropical night air. Then, we shook hands and wished each other a good night.

CHAPTER 16
The Soul of the "Chichibu Maru"

For more than a week now, our ship raced towards Japan – yet our destination still seemed as far away as ever. A few impatient passengers uttered similar opinion. One said that the captain had mentioned Japan was still many thousand kilometers ahead! We all gained a new respect for the vastness of this Silent Sea!

The Hawaiian Islands was approximately halfway across the enormous stretch between America and Japan, which we reached in the span of a week, sailing forward day and night at the highest speed. It could only be one more week before we saw land.

While I pondered this, one of the ship's officers passed me. I asked: "How much farther now to Japan?"

Nonni in Japan

"Eight to nine thousand kilometers," replied the officer. "It will be at least one more week."

I could understand that some were getting weary. For their part, the Japanese captain and his officers did all they could to see that every day had something new. For one thing, a little newspaper was published daily with information broadcast over the radio waves with news and novelties from around the world.

I enjoyed the untiring friendliness of the Japanese boy for many of these hours. He was well informed about almost everything happening on board, and he never missed telling me what I might find interesting. For instance, long after the Hawaiian Islands disappeared from our eyes, leaving us only with the sky and the vast expanse of the ocean, he said: "Today, something nice will be shown to us!"

"And how do you know this, dear child?" I asked him.

"From the captain himself," he replied confidently. "A short while ago, I heard him talking with his men, saying that he would show the big machine room to any passengers interested in seeing it. We should go have a look!"

I accepted his invitation, of course, and we joined a rather large number of passengers following guides to the machine room in the lower portion of the ship.

The nearer we got to the mighty room, the louder and scarier came the noises from therein. At last, we reached the entrance to the mysteries that lie behind the door. The captain stopped and waited until all passengers were standing close together. Then he said: "We will soon enter, but first, I want to advise you that the machine room bears a certain danger, so please, be careful."

Nonni in Japan

The captain opened the door. A great heat struck us, but then, we beheld a long and wide hall full of machines at work. Many narrow pathways wound in all directions. To both right and left were wheels big and small rotating at unbelievable speed. Between them were heavy iron bars moving curiously: some continuously stomped up and down at lightning-fast speed. Others, moved incessantly to and fro. Everything in that fairy-like room was moving, creating whistling and roaring noises everywhere. It was impossible to have any conversation; all one could hear was this "concert" of whirring, wildly noisy, rumbling wheels and bars.

The captain went in front of us as our guide. He shouted over the din: "Everything here, the wheels and bars and all the other pieces – has only one purpose, which is to move our ship forward. These engines work nonstop, day by day, week by week. If ever they should fail, our ship would be a dead mass, motionless on the ocean. For that reason, we maintain our machines with utmost care. Those machines are the heart — or better still, the soul — of the ship!" We lingered a short while more as the captain heard and answered numerous questions from the fascinated passengers.

When we returned to the deck, my young friend impressed me with his manners, saying, "I have been sure to thank the officers for being so willing with their explanations. Now, I intend to thank the captain for being so friendly and showing us the machine room!"

Nonni in Japan

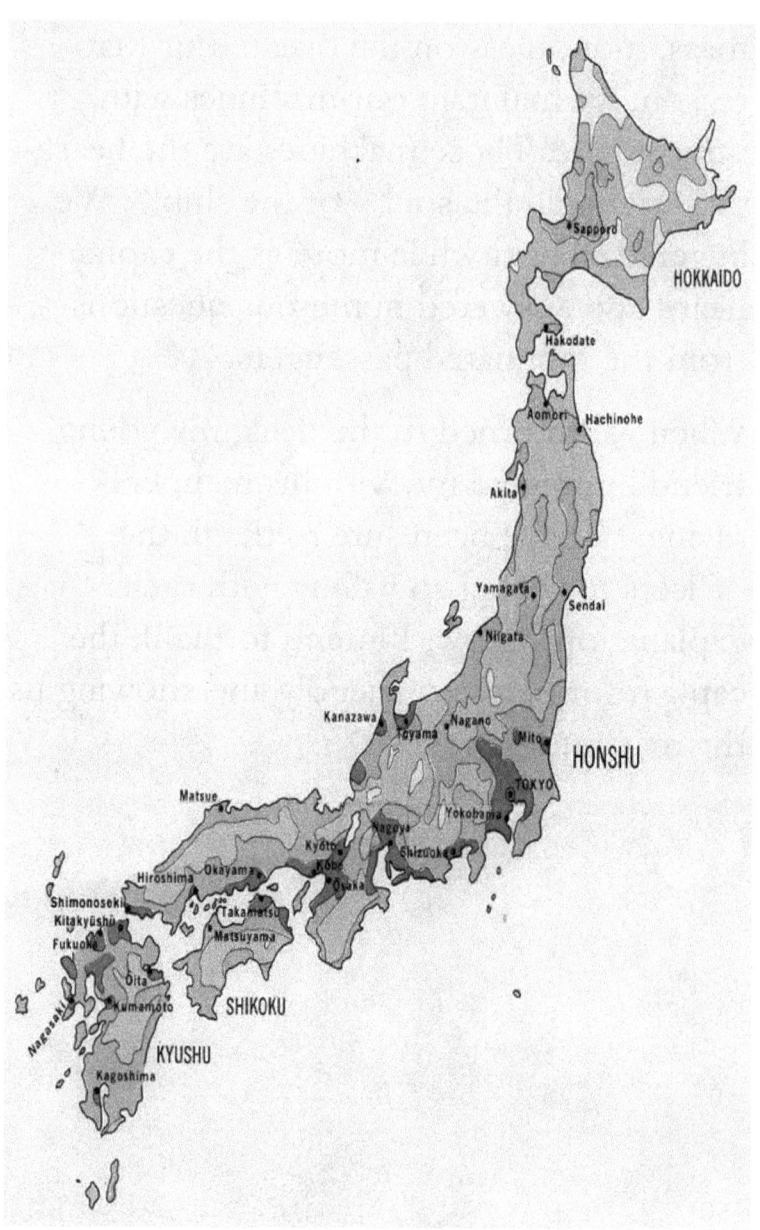

Nonni in Japan

CHAPTER 17
My Little Friend Speaks of Japan

I felt my little Japanese friend had a reasonable point, and so I went with him in order to thank the captain. After our "field trip," we went back to the deck and the vast quietness of the Pacific Ocean – quite a contrast to the cacophony of the machines powering the ship!

"Isn't it strange," began the little Japanese boy, "that we have been steaming onward across this great ocean for quite some time now and have not yet met a single ship?"

"Yes, I have been wondering about that," I replied. "I have seen none, except for the American war ships near the Hawaiian Islands. That is rather strange."

The boy said: "As we approach Japan, we shall see many more ships."

Nonni in Japan

"What sort of ships will these be?" I asked. "Will they be steamers, or sailing boats?"

"Some small steamers, but mostly sailing boats," he answered. "They are the fishing fleet of Japan, great in number and often rather far from the coast."

"Why so many?" I asked the boy.

"That part of the country is very densely populated," he replied.

Then the boy explained further: "Our ship will land in the city of Yokohama, which is a very large city with almost one million inhabitants. Not far from there is the city of Kobe, which is about the same size; and then there is Tokyo, the capital of Japan. Tokyo has approximately six million inhabitants and lies relatively near Kobe and Yokohama. Altogether, many millions of people live in that small part of Japan where our ship will arrive."

Nonni in Japan

The boy continued: "Tokyo is one of the largest cities of the whole world, though I believe that London and New York are larger. And, as the Japanese eat more fish than meat, a very large fishing fleet is necessary, as you will soon see!"

As my intelligent little friend continued, he sounded more like an adult than a small boy! I commented: "If Tokyo has six million inhabitants, it must be larger than Paris, Berlin, or Vienna. I would hardly have thought that possible!"

"I am absolutely sure that this is true," he assured me. "Tokyo is the third largest city of the world; I learnt that at school! I also learnt that Tokyo has a diameter of more than thirty kilometers."

"But…" I began, "… are you not mistaken, my dear friend? A diameter of thirty kilometers would be enormous!"

"No, I am not mistaken!" He was silent as he pondered a few moments, then said:

Nonni in Japan

"Thirty-five. Tokyo has a diameter of thirty-five kilometers."

It seemed to me hardly possible, impossibly large. But my friend insisted his teacher said thirty-five kilometers, and I believed him. "I shall have to examine this myself!" I spoke.

"Then you will be convinced, indeed," he responded.

A few Japanese sailors came along, and the boy addressed them in his native language. It seemed that he asked them a favor. Of course, I did not understand a single word. The sailors answered him in the same language and went away.

I asked the boy what he had talked about with the sailors.

He replied: "I asked how many days until we reach Japan."

"What did they answer?"

"It will still be a couple of days before we land in Yokohama."

"So, then, we are closer to the end of our long voyage," I remarked.

"Yes, in two days," he said. Then he added: "I have heard that the captain will give us a big festive dinner tomorrow – not in the dining room, but right here, on deck!"

"That might be our farewell meal," I commented.

"Yes, probably," replied the boy. "For this occasion, the captain gives a gift to each passenger."

"My!" I exclaimed. "I have never seen anything like that done in Europe!"

"That is the custom on many Japanese ships," said the boy. "The farewell meal will have magnificent decorations of flowers and flags. In the evening, the whole deck will be illuminated, and when the meal is over, there will be a splendid fireworks display."

CHAPTER 18
A Farewell Meal with Japan in Sight

Everything did indeed happen according to the Japanese boy's description. The farewell meal was quite festive and the presents very special.

The captain's gifts had been placed next to the plate of every guest, whose names were written on place cards, to avoid any confusion. Many were astonished that the captain went to such expense. Our presents consisted of small Japanese items. I received a pair of cute chopsticks, for example.

During the meal, the deck was brilliantly illuminated. There were also Japanese musicians playing from time to time. A variety of films were being shown for those who desired such entertainments. In short, everything was provided to keep us in good

Nonni in Japan

spirits, and all my table companions appreciated these gestures.

After the meal, my little Japanese friend informed me that we would see Japan the following day. So, this would be the last day of our long voyage across the Silent Sea! I was not sure if I would see my inseparable travel companion after this meal, so I took that moment to thank him from the bottom of my heart for the friendship he had shown me throughout the entire voyage. He claimed it was me who deserved HIS gratitude!

After the meal everybody went out on deck, where the night was warm and pitch-black. No breeze was stirring. And then, the fireworks began! It looked as if flames and glowing stars were being tossed into the air as the whole ship emitted fiery blazes of light!

Among the passengers there were a few French speaking travelers who exclaimed:

Nonni in Japan

"*Magnifique…! Splendide…! Jamais nous n'avons rien vu de semblable à Paris…!*" (Magnificent…! Splendid…! We have never seen anything like that in Paris…!)

When this brilliant performance concludec, the boy grabbed me by the arm and said: "Will you please come with me?"

"Where do you want to lead me, dear child?" I asked.

"You will see in a moment."

"Yes, I will go with you!"

He guided me into a brightly illuminated hall, where many people sat at nice little tables. I was brought to a group of Japanese ladies and gentlemen. The boy whispered into my ear: "My parents and a few friends of ours are there."

A gentleman and a lady got up and approached me.

They bowed and said to me in English: "We are the parents of your little friend!" Then they added: "We want to thank you for your friendliness toward our son. He has been a persistent companion, no doubt!"

I answered: "You need not thank me for anything. Yes, your little boy has often visited me. He has never been a bother, but always brought me joy."

They asked me to have a seat, where I was met with more rounds of praise and niceties. They wanted to celebrate my farewell to their son – not just with their words, but even with real champagne and other delicacies!

"It is our last evening together," said the father. "Tomorrow we shall land in Yokohama."

Although I did not find out the names of those loveable people, I at least knew that they were going on to Tokyo, like me. However, they would be there only for a

Nonni in Japan

short while. I sat for quite a while in that pleasant company, but finally it was time to go to rest. We parted as good friends and went to our cabins.

The following day I was up a bit earlier than usual. When I had dressed and was done with the day's preparations, I went on deck. The weather was sunny and clear.

I chose a quiet place on the highest deck. There I took my binoculars out of my pocket and looked ahead. There was hardly anything special to be seen. However, to the left I noticed several steamships and sailing boats lying still on the water. This was the big fishing fleet at work!

To the right I only saw the endless vastness of the Silent Sea.

When I looked ahead through the binoculars once more, it seemed to me that in the far distance there might be land. But it was so unclear – because it was so far away – that I could not make out what it was.

Nonni in Japan

While I was standing there, I heard a familiar voice behind me calling "Good morning!"

I turned around and discovered my little friend. He jumped over to me quickly, pointed and said: "Can you see anything ahead?"

"I can hardly discern anything," I said. "But it seems that there is a coast… and that must be Japan."

"Yes, that is Japan. And the city we will soon see at the shore is Yokohama, where we shall land."

Then he pointed to the left and asked: "Can you see the many ships there?"

I did see more and more clearly the many steamers and sailing boats lying there, motionless.

"Yes! Are these the Japanese fishing fleet about which we talked the other day?"

Nonni in Japan

He answered in the affirmative, and then he was called away by his parents.

Nonni in Japan

CHAPTER 19
Seeing an Imperial Japanese Prince

Shortly afterwards, my friend raced back with a beaming face and said: "I have news for you!"

I looked at him searchingly.

He continued: "In a few minutes, we shall pass several big Japanese ships. On the main ship are two of the highest and most noble personalities of Japan – namely, the prince and the princess Chichibu! Our ship bears that name, as you know! They belong to the Imperial Japanese family and are on their way to England to attend the coronation of the English king. The Imperial ship of the prince and the princess will pass very closely by us, and during that moment, we passengers shall greet them with a loud 'Banzai!'"

I was not surprised at all when shortly afterwards we were summoned to the highest deck. The loudspeaker announced: "May all passengers please gather there to see the Imperial couple Chichibu, and salute them when they pass by on their ship."

The passengers gladly complied as the ship of the Imperial couple drew closer and closer. We could already see both Imperial persons quite clearly. They, too, were standing on top of the highest deck of their magnificent ship.

Now they were there! Opposite us! In the immediate vicinity!

We took off our hats and caps, waving to the Imperial couple as we shouted "Banzai!"

The Imperial couple waved back kindly… and thus, our homage had been performed with the highest dignity. Several Japanese boats accompanied the imperial ship on their voyage to London.

After the Imperial ship passed us, my little Japanese friend returned to point out a few

Nonni in Japan

more things. On the left, the big Japanese fishing fleet was still at work. There were many big and small steamboats as well as sailing boats. I was amazed at their size, and their number.

The boy reminded me: "You must not forget that they have to fish for many millions of people."

While my friend previously informed me about the number of inhabitants of Tokyo and a few other Japanese cities, he drew my attention this time to the population of the entire Japanese empire.

"The number of inhabitants of Japan is rising considerably. A few years ago, Japan only had forty to sixty million inhabitants. Now, there are approximately eighty million."

Then, he continued, with pride: "Japan consists of a few large islands and many small ones, you know."

"Yes," I said. "I have often heard and read about them. Could you please tell me the names of some of the islands, so that I can write them down to remember? I would love to get some information on their surroundings as well."

The boy answered: "I know the names of the big islands because we had to learn them at school. The largest of the islands is the one on which we shall land. It is called 'Nippon'! Tokyo, the capital of Japan, is situated on this island. There are a few more big cities on this island. The entire island of Nippon has between forty to fifty million inhabitants."

"Forty to fifty million!" I cried in surprise. "Is that correct?"

"Yes, I am sure!" he promised. "The second largest island is called 'Jesso' and has approximately three million inhabitants. Then, there is the island 'Kiuschiu' with nine to ten million inhabitants. Finally, there is the last big island is 'Schikoku,' which has about four million inhabitants. These are the four large islands of Japan."

"Are these then the most important islands of Japan?"

"Yes, these are the most important and the largest islands. But there are, of course the smaller ones…"

"They probably do not have much to say, do they?"

"Oh, yes! Judging by their size they might not have much to say, but because of their immensely great numbers they do have plenty. I don't know their names by heart because there are so many."

"I cannot expect that from you after all," I assured him. "But maybe you know how many of those smaller islands there are in Japan?"

The boy replied: "I only know that there are very many."

"Can you say an approximate number, at least? —Are there twenty, thirty or perhaps one hundred of such small islands?"

"Twenty, thirty or one hundred?" he answered. "Oh, no, there are many more! I know for sure that there are far more than five hundred small Japanese islands. And I also know for sure that together they have almost one million inhabitants."

I was astonished that the little boy knew so much about his fatherland. I asked him: "Little friend, do you have to learn all that at school? And how can you remember everything so well?"

"Oh," he said, "All boys of my age know these facts."

Meanwhile our ship continued its approach to the island of Nippon. That is where Yokohama is situated and – as mentioned before – the splendid capital of Tokyo, where I was going to stay.

Nonni in Japan

The boy took me by the hand and led me to the railing of the ship from where one had the best view ahead.

He pointed with his hand straight ahead and asked me: "Can you see the huge ships over there?"

"Yes, I can see them very well. They are much bigger than the ones we have seen so far."

"Yes! Do you know what kind of ships they are?"

"No, I don't know. Do they perhaps belong to the great fishing fleet over there?"

"Oh no, these are ships which accompanied the prince and princess Chichibu. Now they are returning to their location."

I was very astonished and exclaimed: "Does Japan really have so many huge ships? I had no idea. Where are they built?"

"I don't know where they are built. And I don't know how many there are."

I was extremely astonished when I saw all those proud ships and began to count them.

As I was taking a few notes, a gentleman came by. He stopped near me and said: "We do not allow passengers to take any notes here, and especially no photographs, as the coast is fortified."

I put my notebook back into my pocket immediately. I had not travelled to Japan as a spy, after all. My goal was exactly the opposite!

Nonni in Japan

Nonni in Japan

CHAPTER 20
Landing in Japan While Thinking of Home

As we drew closer and closer to the Japanese coast, I prepared myself for our imminent landing in Yokohama by saying good-bye to the passengers with whom I had made friends, beginning with the little Japanese boy. The bonds between us were loosened not without great emotion!

I also packed up my belongings and locked them in my suitcases.

So it was that I now turned my full attention toward entering that country which I spent most of my life imagining, and now was about to see in person.

Our approach was slow and calm. At last, we drew so near the coast that we could distinguish between the people and things we could see. I grew very excited thinking I was about to put my foot on Asian ground for the first time! In just a few more

Nonni in Japan

minutes, I would be in that country on the opposite side of the globe! I pictured the earth, that immensely big ball, and thought of that conversation with my mother, seventy years earlier, on the farm of Möðruvellir. This is when she showed me the globe and explained, to my amazement, that the earth was round like a ball and that there were completely new countries and oceans when one spun the ball to see the other side. I realized I was now separated from my fatherland by the entire breadth of that sphere. I was the same distance from Iceland, whether I went forward or backward! For seventy years, I longed to see the countries on the other side of the earth… and today, my wish was about to become true: I had really arrived at the other side of that ball!

We eased toward the city of Yokohama, where I was to go ashore, but that is not where I would stay during my visit. From Yokohama I would head further into the

Nonni in Japan

country until reaching Tokyo. There, I would settle at a university which had been founded (and still was run) by German scholars. The Japanese name of that university is "Jochi Daigaku," with its address "Kojimachi Kioicho." I had sent ahead the details of my arrival by letter from America.

I knew that Tokyo was not very far from Yokohama, but I did not know the exact distance. One of my companions on the "Chichibu Maru" said it was between twenty and thirty kilometers. I wondered how I should cover that stretch, particularly with my suitcases. I had no idea, after all, about the modes of local transportation. As I pondered this matter, a senior Japanese traveler passed by. Thankfully, he spoke some English. I asked: "Excuse me, Sir, could you please tell me how I can get from Yokohama to Tokyo with my suitcases?"

After a pause, he said: "The best way is to go by car."

"Is it easy to get a car, or horse-drawn carriage, in Yokohama?" I asked.

"There are both," he answered. "But you might also consider going by rickshaw."

A rickshaw? – What might that be? I thought to myself.

The Japanese gentleman saw that I was at a loss, but persisted: "In Yokohama, you will find rickshaws, or jin rickshaws, without any problem."

Seeing that I had no idea what he meant, the gentleman said: "A rickshaw, or jin rickshaw, is a very light carriage for people that is drawn by a servant. In other words, they are carriages are not drawn by horses, but by men."

Astonished, I asked, "Men draw travelers in carriages? Do I understand correctly? How is this possible?"

Nonni in Japan

"They do so without difficulty because the carriages are very light and the roads are in good shape," he explained. "The carriages have two large and extremely light wheels. You will have no trouble finding a rickshaw in Yokohama."

I thanked the gentleman and resolved to ride in a rickshaw, if possible.

At that moment, our steamer entered the port of Yokohama. At the quay, the "Chichibu Maru" was fastened to the bulwark. Several landing stages were placed between shore and ship, and people began boarding our ship from land. I supposed they were friends and acquaintances of some of the passengers. Soon, there was a big crowd of people on the deck. I remained unknown in the midst of the multitude.

I turned to one of my European travel companions and asked him: "Are these people coming on board Japanese?" He cast an attentive and inquiring glance at the large crowd of people surrounding us, and said: "Yes, these are mostly Japanese. However, there are also a few Chinese among them." He drew my attention to some of the differences between these two peoples.

"Can you see the two gentlemen over there, having an eager conversation with each other?"

I had a close look and saw them instantly. "I have found them," I replied.

"Very well. The one on the right is Chinese. You can tell by his face, and his nuances. The Chinese are typically a little taller than the Japanese, on the whole; and, the Japanese tend to gesture more when they speak than do the Chinese."

Nonni in Japan

Nonni in Japan

Nonni in Japan

CHAPTER 21
How I was Received in Japan - Arrival in Tokyo

Landing in Japan felt like being on a stage, with my surroundings comprising the show: the people, the sounds, and the customs felt new and strange. Even the colors and the air around me felt different!

I began to feel forlorn. But suddenly, and strangely enough, I heard from behind me someone call: "*Guten Tag, Nonni* (Good day, Nonni)!"

Was I dreaming? Or was it true? I turned around to see four gentlemen looking at me kindly. I cast them an inquiring look, not recognizing any of them. Their attire was European, but only three were European faces; the fourth was Japanese. One wore a strikingly nice but peculiar beard, rather full around the mouth so that it covered his chin completely. The other three gentlemen were clean-shaven: two, nearly juvenile; the other, elderly. All four were extremely polite and dignified in demeanor.

When they came nearer, I said: "I don't know how to thank you for your friendly welcome. Nor do I know who you are, or from where you come!"

"We have come from Tokyo to pick you up and bring you to Jochi Daigaku University!" they announced.

"But – how do you know that I have come on 'Chichibu Maru'?" I asked.

They answered heartily, "You detailed your arrival by letter from California. We knew on which ship you would come and where you would land in Japan."

"Yes," I answered. "But it is a wonder you recognized me among such a multitude of passengers! I see you know my name, but I don't know yours, unfortunately."

"My name is Keel, and I am Swiss," said the one standing immediately next to me.

Nonni in Japan

"You live in Tokyo?"

"Yes, I am employed at Jochi Daigaku University."

The second gentleman then shook my hand and said: "My name is Yoshio Kobayaschi, and I am from Japan."

I would later learn that Mr. Kobayaschi was a famous scholar and writer, and a professor at Jochi Daigaku University. He had sailed on the training ship "Wanimaru" to the Philippines in his youth, and, like Robinson, had passed many adventures. He wrote about his journey in a beautiful book entitled "Wanimaru," which saw the light of day in the same publishing house as the Nonni books. I also learned that Mr. Kobayaschi had studied European culture in the same community to which my own travel companion Viktor belonged (… Viktor accompanied me on my second trip to Iceland which I described in the book

Nonni in Japan

"Die Feuerinsel im Nordmeer" / "The fiery island in the North Sea").

The third gentleman said: "My name is Rupert Enderle. I am German, and I belong to the Herder publishing house in Freiburg im Breisgau. I am from their school of apprentices, and I am acquainted with your former companion, Viktor. When I was nineteen, I left my home in Germany with a rucksack on my back and eight Reichsmark in my pocket. I took the trans-Siberian railroad for weeks through Russian cities, wasteland, and woods, as far as Wladiwostok on the Sea of Japan. From there I traveled by ship to Tokyo, where I have established a publishing house and a library. I work part-time as a lecturer at Jochi Daigaku University."

Suddenly, an image came into my mind. "Have we not already met in Freiburg?" I asked Mr. Enderle. It seemed to me that I had met that tall and strikingly agile young man before.

"Certainly, yes," answered the young German. "We have met several times. Before I left Germany, I ran the reading hour for children at Herder's in Freiburg, and I organized Nonni events there. You talked to children about your adventures on two such occasions."

"Ah! I was not mistaken – we do know each other already!" I greeted my young friend from Germany a second time. "Now I remember those lively hours when I told stories from my life to children of the employees of Herder. A tall young man kept the fidgety children in check so that I had the chance to speak."

"Yes, that's right," my young friend confirmed. "That's how I recognized you and called you 'Nonni.' Furthermore, I've edited two 'Nonni' books in Japanese here

Nonni in Japan

in Tokyo, in my publishing house, so that Nonni may be known in Japan, too."

Finally, the fourth gentleman said: "My name is Schwak, and I am German, too. I am also employed at Jochi Daigaku University."

I felt rather comfortable in that circle of Europeans amidst the Asian world and was about to entrust my needs to these four men, when yet another gentleman approached, heartily calling me "Nonni." No, I was not mistaken!

"Nonni! Hello! My name is Franz Diesch. I am Viktor's younger brother – Viktor, who accompanied you to Iceland – and I work at Herder publishing house in Japan."

I shook hands with the brave boy, barely eighteen years old, with the Swabian German dialect. I remarked that he resembled Viktor like one egg to another. His accent sounded comfortably familiar in this unfamiliar Asian atmosphere!

"How on earth have you found me?" I asked the pleasant young man curiously.

"I am part of this party too," he answered. "Only, I was at the other end of the dock, in case you might be found in the middle of the ship, or on deck, or anywhere else." He was obviously very practical. "I am glad we found you quickly!" he continued. "But now we should pick up your luggage so that we can take it to the train station. We are not in a hurry, but we need not waste too much time."

My suitcases which stood nearby were gathered and carried ashore. From that moment on, I did not have to worry about anything: my competent and very amiable young friends took care of my needs in the best way.

We left the ship and went to the train station nearby, with my helpers carrying my belongings into the train.

Nonni in Japan

I paused in astonishment in the doorway to take in the beautiful, elegant, and comfortable railway carriage, sparkling with cleanliness. I found a nice seat and sat down.

Soon the beautiful train took off in a rush towards Tokyo.

Now and then, I caught sight of small farms, rice plantations, and a few trees and bushes here and there. Shortly, a few uniformed Japanese railway officials entered our car through the door on one end.

"They are ticket inspectors," said my neighbor. "You will want to notice their behavior," he added in a low voice.

The two men locked the door behind them. They remained at the door for a few moments, took off their caps and greeted the passengers politely with a few Japanese words. Then they went to each passenger, made a quick bow, and checked the tickets.

Nonni in Japan

"Do you know what they had said when standing at the door?" asked my neighbor. "They begged our pardon for taking the liberty to check our tickets!"

"How is it that they are so polite?" I asked.

"The Japanese are the politest people in the world, without any doubt," was his answer.

Suddenly it got darker. I looked out of the window and noticed our surroundings had changed completely. The train began to slow down. On both sides of the track there appeared houses and parks.

"This is Tokyo," said my neighbor. "In a few minutes we shall enter Tokyo station."

Of course, I was curious, and looked attentively through the window.

It got darker and darker as the train slid into a huge station. It was full of people, and several long trains were beside us. It was clear that we had entered a city of millions.

Nonni in Japan

"Tokyo!" shouted a strong voice from somewhere.

"We are here!" shouted my friends.

We got off, and I was immersed in the great crowd at Tokyo train station.

Nonni in Japan

Nonni in Japan

Nonni in Japan

CHAPTER 22
My First Impressions of Tokyo

Yes, here we were in the capital of Japan, the third biggest city of the world, and by far, the biggest city in all of Asia!

We were to leave the train station by car under the guidance of my friends, driving through the mighty city of Tokyo up to Jochi Daigaku University, where I was to live during my stay in Japan. I very eagerly looked forward to that ride!

One of my companions signaled a chauffeur, and almost instantly, a car pulled up towards us. I was astonished to see how quickly, easily, and safely that happened. My suitcases were fetched from the train and handed over to the chauffeur. Before I got in the car, I cast a few curious looks around me. The train station looked very much like those in European cities. There were trains to the left and to the right, and everything was very modern. Japan was certainly up to date in terms of progress and technical accomplishments.

Some of the Japanese men in the crowd wore clothes I might have seen in Europe. All Japanese women, however, wore their own uniquely traditional attire. I liked their clothing very much. It also struck me that Japanese women carried their small children and babies on their backs, in a sort of wrap – not in arms, as European mothers do. These carrying shawls are so skillfully folded that only the little heads of the children are visible behind the mother's shoulder. Thus, Japanese mothers could move about freely, and their little ones seemed comfortable. The babies seldom cried, as far as I could see; they were able to sleep soundly and calmly in their swaddle. One might think the mothers oblivious to the bundles on their backs, so energetically did they clamber about. Later, I would learn that older siblings sometimes carried younger brothers

Nonni in Japan

and sisters on their backs, in similar fashion. When there was an older boy without sisters, he was obliged to carry the sibling on his back. This rule only applies to boys younger than ten, I learned; older boys are released from such obligation and earn the right to command their sisters – and even their mothers.

Of course, if the little ones wrapped in back began to cry, their carriers could do very little, and the babes were expected to settle themselves. I wondered if the Japanese cultural practice of bearing hardships patiently and without protest develops during the time spent in these back-carriers!

When I and my suitcases were in the car, we set out to Jochi Daigaku University. I was about to see the streets of this big Asian city for the first time!

Near the train station, the houses were big and palatial like those in most European cities. Everything was magnificent and metropolitan. Further out, however, came the suburbs and the less affluent homes. As is true everywhere in the world, there are a few with much wealth, but the many are simpler in their lifestyles – and those are the bearers of the customs and traditions, and the genuine face of a nation's people. While the area around the railway station felt like a deliberate and progressive imitation of European style, the less extravagant areas found the Japanese-Asian culture in bloom, lovingly tended and as reverently guarded now as it was a thousand years ago. Here is where people depend on one another by the same creed; where they know each other well, and where nature itself – fields and woods, wind and weather – is an important neighbor. It is true in Iceland that some believe they have advanced beyond the effects of the forces of nature, and such people seem detached from the thoughts and feelings of the common folk. Yet, the darker the days grow, and the deeper we

Nonni in Japan

become buried by snow, the closer we move together on our farms – and the more pronounced become our Icelandic traditions.

Those lovely memories arose in me as we passed the cute, single-story houses. What struck me most was the presence of a little garden in front of every house —each with some swatch of nature, be this a tiny tree, a flower, or just a bit of grass. I asked one of my companions about the gardens. He answered: "Yes, this is typical design. Each house has room for one family, or two at the most, but without fail, there must be a garden. The Japanese consider it indispensable to have something living and growing outside each house. The garden must be prominent, even if there is only one square foot or two of earth in which to plant. At the very least, a small tree can take root. Nearly anything can be represented in miniature: a meadow, a forest, a creek, a mountain, a valley… even a bridge.

Nonni in Japan

Sometimes, a small stone is enough to recall the image of the mountains." I found the Japanese love of nature very touching!

As I pondered each small garden sanctuary, I noticed our surroundings beginning to change. The streets began to broaden, with houses placed right up to the edge. These houses had space in back, with big, beautiful gardens tended with care and diligence. The houses were bigger, and trees stood in long rows alongside the sidewalks. There was more traffic, too, like in European cities.

At last, my companions announced we were at our destination. I saw a rather big building. It was Jochi Daigaku, the Japanese University which had been founded by German scholars some years before.

When we stopped in front of the entrance, we left the car and entered the university building.

Nonni in Japan

Nonni in Japan

CHAPTER 23
I am Welcomed at Jochi Daigaku University and Meet Professor Hermann Heuvers

I was received with great politeness at the entrance to Jochi Daigaku University. A young Japanese employee guided me to a small waiting-room, kindly offering me a chair and making signs to wait there a little while. With a few English words, more signs, a vocal intonation, and a smile, he conveyed I would be introduced shortly to the rector. Then, he made a deep bow and left the room.

As I waited, I pondered. *At last, I am finally in the wonderland Japan*, I thought to myself. *Today a new life is beginning for me! I have finally covered half of the way around the globe… and I shall stay in this wonderland for at least a year! How will I be received and treated at the university, with most of my hosts and students being Japanese? How shall I understand the Japanese and their culture? What will occupy me during my stay? And,*

Nonni in Japan

what will be the wonders awaiting me in this magnificent country?

Thoughts and images buzzed in my mind. I had already read a lot about Japan and the Japanese culture, and I knew many beautiful things about this country. But it was entirely different to get to know this splendid place in person, with my own eyes!

A knock on the door interrupted my thoughts. I quickly called in English, "Come in!"

The smiling employee entered once again. "If you please, come with me," he said politely. "I shall accompany you to the director of the university, as the rector is not at home."

As we went into the corridor, I asked my guide, "What is the name of the university director?"

"His name is Heuvers," replied my companion.

"And, the name of the rector?"

"The rector's name is Roggen," he said. "He is the superior of the whole house. Director Heuvers," he added, "is responsible for everything concerning university instruction and science. Rector Roggen is responsible for the rest."

I tried to memorize both names: Roggen and Heuvers.

Heuvers would be a highly scholarly gentleman, a man of the highest sciences. I felt a deep respect toward him, along with a certain shyness in meeting such a learned scholar.

After we had walked through several corridors we passed a large map of a big city. I asked my guide which city that was.

"This is Tokyo," he said.

"It is quite large," I remarked. "How many citizens live there?"

"Around six million."

"Do you happen to know how wide it is?"

"The diameter is about 35 kilometers."

"In that case, Tokyo is one of the biggest cities of the world."

"Yes, that's correct," said the young man. "They say that it is the third largest city of the world."

By now we arrived at a flight of stairs. My guide gestured we would ascend, and so we did, entering a new corridor with many doors.

"The rector of the house and university director live here, as well as several professors," said the young usher.

We continued a few steps to the right and stopped in front of one of the doors. He said in a low voice: "This is the room of director Heuvers" as he knocked on the door.

Nonni in Japan

"Come in," was the answer from inside.

My companion opened the door and announced: "Here is our European guest."

I entered the room. A tall, imposing gentleman approached me with a friendly smile. He stretched both arms towards me and exclaimed: "Oh, here he is! Welcome, Nonni!" He repeated his welcome several times, grabbing my hands most kindly and then offering me a chair. I was so moved by his heartfelt reception that I could hardly utter a word. Mr. Heuvers, Director of Jochi Daigaku University, was both one of the most scholarly and most amiable persons I have met in my life.

I sat with him for a long time and answered many questions. When we concluded, he offered to take me to meet Rector Roggen, who by now had returned. He, too, welcomed me most kindly, just like Director Heuvers, assuring me I could stay as long as I wished.

Nonni in Japan

"You must remain with us at least one year," he said. "You will need that time if you want to get to know Japan and the Japanese better." He added: "The Japanese tend to keep to themselves, so as to not trouble others, so it will take some time to become acquainted with them."

Rector Roggen then led me to the room reserved for my stay in Tokyo. It was the best room of the university – the room where his predecessor, University Rector Hoffmann, had lived. I must admit that I had not expected such treatment, and I was almost ashamed to see such exquisite provisions offered to me. And yet, this is the reception given me by Rector Roggen and Director Heuvers, for however long I was to stay at the university!

Although Director Heuvers had a full schedule most days, he accompanied me numerous times through Tokyo and other Japanese cities where, under his guidance, I would give lectures in schools and educational institutions with the help of interpreters. He even managed to lead me into the imperial palace of the Mikado – into the famous island fortress where His Majesty the Emperor of Japan resided, the sublime and revered Tenno! But, I will tell more about that later.

Nonni in Japan

Nonni in Japan

CHAPTER 24
My First Day at Jochi Daigaku University

That first day, I had lunch with a group of university professors, some other university inhabitants, and employees. Afterward, I found myself feeling tired, especially with all these new impressions and introductions. Therefore, I retreated to my room to rest. But, my thoughts had a hard time settling!

It is so wonderful… I have traveled over half of the surface of the earth and have arrived at the opposite side of the globe! And that long journey has taken a half year already!

In seven months, I have traveled across the Atlantic Ocean, crossed the New World, and then crossed the Pacific Ocean to Japan, the fairytale land I dreamed of since childhood! I will stay at least one full year in this empire of Eastern Asia, with the people about whom I have read so much, and whom the missionary Francis Xavier praised and loved as the

Nonni in Japan

most talented people he met during his travels around the world. How can I be so lucky?

It was hard to rest. And then, there was knocking at my door. *Ah… this will be my fate in Japan, too*, I thought to myself. I straightened up in the recliner and shouted my famous "Come in!".

A young man stepped in, smiling obligingly but remaining in the doorway.

"Good day, good day!" I called towards him, smiling and getting up to greet him.

He seized my outstretched hand and asked in English: "I'm not disturbing you?"

"No, not at all!" I answered, guiding him to my table and dragging a chair towards him.

Smiling, he sat down. Then followed a conversation in English:

"I have heard," he began, "that you come from Iceland. Is that so?"

"Yes," I replied. "I am an Icelander, born in Iceland. However, I didn't travel here from Iceland, but from the European mainland, where I have been living for many years."

"I see… you don't live in Iceland anymore. Do you still speak Icelandic?"

"Certainly! Not only is Icelandic my mother tongue, but it is also a beautiful classic language."

"Yes, I know. I, too, am very much interested in Icelandic and Icelandic literature."

I could hardly believe my ears. I expected him to have never heard of Iceland!

"Do tell me," I said, incredulously, "how it is you have such interest in Iceland and Icelandic literature!"

"As student, I have studied English. If, however, one wants to learn English well, one must know the roots from which English is derived, including Icelandic."

"Where can you study Icelandic here in Japan?" I asked.

"Our Imperial University here in Tokyo has a very competent professor of Icelandic literature. He teaches English, Icelandic, and Icelandic literature. I have not studied there, but a friend of mine has studied English and Icelandic with Professor Ichikawa, a master of both languages. That friend has taught me the little bit I know about Icelandic. But, it is not much," he added modestly.

I knew that the Imperial University in Tokyo had a high reputation among the great universities worldwide. It seemed quite natural for English and Icelandic to be taught there. But, to be absolutely sure, I asked my new Japanese friend a few questions about Old Norse Mythology. I asked him how Odin, Thor, Loki, and Freya were dealt with in the Edda. He passed my mini examination with flying colors! He also knew Helgi Hundingsbani and other details

Nonni in Japan

from the Edda. I was still quite astonished by his interest in the mythology of the old Icelandic literature.

During our conversation, I also learned various interesting details of his own circumstances. Although he was a student, he was very poor – so poor that he could only afford one meal per day! To earn money, he worked as a streetcar driver on one of the many trams of Tokyo. He drove the tram four hours each day, and his wage was sufficient for one solid meal every twenty-four hours. And yet, he was satisfied with it. He spent the remaining hours of the day studying, often staying up until midnight each evening. Very seldom did he get to bed earlier. It seemed the Japanese thirst for knowledge transcended all other things.

Then he shared that he had a great desire to travel to Iceland to see the country from which the Edda, the sagas and the Old Norse literature arose. Oh, if only I had been wealthy, I would have gladly helped him undertake that trip!

While we were still chatting with each other, there was another knock on my door.

Again, I shouted: "Come in!"

The door opened and a Japanese gentleman stepped in.

The young student got up immediately, made a deep bow, and reached out his hand to say goodbye. He intended to leave, but I surmised the visitor asked him to stay. I could not understand what was spoken as it was all in Japanese. The student, however, politely declined, bowed a few more times, and left the room.

The guest came in, bowed, and asked if he could pay me a short visit. I reached out my hand towards him kindly and said: "Welcome! I am available, of course!"

After he sat down, the visitor began in good English: "I have come from the editorial staff of the Japanese newspapers "Asahi Shimbun" and "Nichi Nichi" to see if you would be willing to write a few short articles for each."

"That sounds easy enough," I replied. "May I ask what the subject will be?"

"The newspapers would like you to tell the readers what you knew and thought about Japan before you came here, and then to comment on the impressions you have now that you have arrived. For your work, the newspapers will offer you 200 Yen." In German currency, that was just over 400 Mark.

"It will be my pleasure," I said.

"Many thanks!" my visitor said. "I look forward to seeing your work!"

Nonni in Japan

CHAPTER 25
What the Japanese Newspaper Man Told Me

I had promised the Japanese newspaper man a few short articles about my impressions of his country.

Not knowing anything about the Japanese newspaper industry, I asked my visitor: "Are the 'Asahi' and 'Nichi-Nichi' prominent papers?"

"Yes, the 'Asahi' and the 'Nichi-Nichi' are two important daily newspapers," he replied.

"How many subscribers do these have?"

"Combined, these two might have three to four million subscribers," answered the man.

I startled when I heard that. Three to four million subscribers, here in Japan? How could that number be correct?

I looked at my visitor for a few moments in silence, as he sat motionless. I repeated my question in other words: "How many copies, then, do you think will be printed of both papers?"

"Three to four million copies are printed daily," answered my visitor. He must have been joking! How could the Japanese have such a booming newspaper industry if they had only been introduced to the American-European culture just one generation ago?

I asked him: "When did the Japanese begin to print daily newspapers?"

"That happened around the year 1870," was the answer.

In that case, I surmised, it took only sixty to seventy years to reach a printing in the millions. The Japanese must be incredibly efficient! My visitor was busy and could only talk a little longer, but I intended to learn more about the Japanese newspaper industry from my hosts, the professors of Jochi Daigaku. When my visitor departed, I went to Director Heuvers with my questions.

"I have heard amazing things about the Japanese newspaper industry," I told him. "But I can never tell if I misunderstand what I hear. I would like to ask you for clarification."

"I am at your disposal," said Director Heuvers.

"What can you tell me about the Japanese Press?" I asked.

He answered in detail: "The Japanese newspaper 'Asahi Shimbun' is edited in Osaka and has assets of six million Yen, which is approximately 12 million Mark. The sister paper is edited in Tokyo and has also assets of six million Yen. Both papers together have a circulation of about three million. A third paper appears in Osaka, called 'Osaka-Mainichi-Shimbun'. That has assets of about ten million Yen, and a circulation of one million. These papers make continuous progress."

I asked: "Are these papers printed in same format as the European newspapers?"

"They are much bigger than the European papers," Director Heuvers answered. "Some papers are issued twice a day: a morning an edition of twelve pages, and an evening edition of eight pages."

"Twelve full pages every morning, and eight every evening! That sounds incredible!" I exclaimed.

"Yes, indeed! But it is true."

My astonishment grew when I was told that the Japanese also founded prominent newspapers in English, for the Europeans. One is called 'The Japan Times;' the other, 'The Japan Mail.' These two papers have a circulation of twenty-five to fifty thousand copies! I marveled at the idea of English newspapers edited in Japan and was amazed by such efficiency.

"Indeed, one has to be amazed thinking about it," said University Director Heuvers. "The Japanese achieve incredibly great things."

He told me that the Japanese newspapers dominate not only the big cities but the whole country. He added: "The extension of the entire Japanese press is extremely generous."

"Where is the center of Japanese press activity?" I asked.

He answered: "The huge paper 'Asahi' – which means 'Morning Sun' – is published simultaneously in Osaka and Tokyo. The paper 'Nichi-Nichi' is published in Tokyo. Both papers are published in several million copies."

"Are 'Asahi' and 'Nichi-Nichi' the only Japanese papers founded so far?"

"No," answered the director. "There are more newspapers in mass circulation, such as the 'Mai Nichi', the 'Yomiuri', the 'Hchi', the 'Nagoya' and the 'Fukuoka'. All of them have their own organization and many employees."

"How many people are employed at each newspaper, would you think?"

"The 'Asahi,' which is published in Tokyo and Osaka, has more than two thousand salaried editors and reporters between the two cities. The other newspapers are similar situation. Each also has hundreds of correspondents in East Asia. Several own fleets of airplanes. 'Asahi' has more than twenty planes, and so they require their own airport."

He continued: "The newspapers also have an impressive number of cars here in Tokyo for driving within the city. One of these days, you will certainly be invited by one or the other of the local papers to take a car ride around the city. Your arrival in Japan has already been announced by the

American papers here. And, as your books are known too, I suspect the local newspapers will bestow on you all sorts of niceties."

Director Heuvers' assumption became true a few days later!

"Besides cars," continued the director, "some papers utilize carrier pigeons to transport articles, photos, and similar information to the editors' offices. The 'Asahi' operates a glider school, and the 'Nichi-Nichi' operates its own amusement park, among other novelties."

"It all sounds fantastic, like a fairytale!" I exclaimed.

"Yes," replied the university director, "it is astonishing to consider, but it is all true."

Only now did I understand what Director Heuvers had strongly emphasized during our conversation: that the big newspapers both dominate the Japanese press and influence the entire country.

Thus, I became acquainted with a Japanese power of the first rank: the press!

Nonni in Japan

CHAPTER 26
I am Invited to a Japanese Theater

The more Japanese people I met, the more I wished to learn about them as a people. Japanese skin is not white like the Europeans,' but a tawny yellowish-brown. Their hair has only one color: namely, dark black. Their facial features are also very different from ours, with a pleasant manner and noble expression. As interesting as these features were to me, I, too, was a sight for the Japanese to see – for, my light skin, white hair and blue eyes were a novelty to behold. Children seemed especially astonished by my appearance. In fact, their interest was so great that one day it led to something quite unexpected.

I was sitting in my room in Jochi Daigaku University when a knock came to my door. What else should I answer but: "Come in!"

Nonni in Japan

A Japanese gentleman stepped in, greeted me with a deep bow and said in English: "Sir, please excuse my disturbing you."

"Please, have a seat. You are not disturbing me at all," I said, dragging a chair towards him.

He said down and said: "Today we are celebrating what we call 'Children's Day' in Japan. That means, we try to please children in a special way. Near here is a theater where we have gathered approximately one thousand children, to show them movies, tell them stories and entertain them for their pleasure. I have come to you asking you a great favor: Will you allow me to take you by car to that theater? It would be an extraordinary delight for the children to see you, and a rare surprise for them to meet with you."

I understood he wished to introduce me on stage to the dear Japanese children. It seemed a bit strange, but also a sweet to be

Nonni in Japan

included in bringing joy to the children and adults gathered in the theater. Why should I not comply – especially as these people loved poets and poetry, sitting for hours in front of their houses on quiet evenings to watch the moon climb over the holy mountain Fujiyama across her vast deep dark celestial arc? Not far from here, in Korea, on the bridge to Japan, there are poets and scholars even in the simple huts in villages. One can find precious old manuscripts and extensive libraries even with common people, and it is considered the greatest honor of a family to have brought forth a poet, and families regularly greet brides and grooms by adorning their houses with fluttering ribbons of poetry. Why should the children not wish to hear stories from my own tales, then?

Hence, I said: "It will be my pleasure to accompany you to see the children. However, I cannot narrate anything, because I know no Japanese."

Nonni in Japan

"Oh, that will not be necessary," said the gentleman. "For the children, it will be a great pleasure simply to see a gentleman storyteller who has come to us from so far."

I saw quite clearly what was expected of me: The children should get the rare pleasure to see a person who had come to them from the other side of the globe, and who looked completely different and who spoke completely different from them. It sounded favorable to me!

During my many wanderings through all continents, I have not found a people who celebrate so many feasts as the Japanese. Each month of the year has its important day, and flowers and blossoms are always in the foreground of each celebration. Arranging a beautiful bouquet is one of the most important tasks of a Japanese woman, and she does so with great solemnity and in her best festive dress. Japanese women arrange flowers with real devotion and great

Nonni in Japan

love, not just as an aside or another ordinary task as in other countries. Hence, it is an extremely beautiful ceremony.

Japanese women decorate their homes like religious people in Christian countries decorate the altars dedicated to Holy Mary in May, with piles of flowers giving off an intense perfume. The people refer to the splendor of flowering trees at home and on the streets, and they pilgrim underneath the trees as if they were holy halls. There is hardly anything more solemn, for instance, than their cherry blossom festival. Their joy far surpasses admiration for natural beauty; you can truly feel something supernatural, something divine.

"How close the Asian people are to us Christians!" I said very often to my friends in Tokyo, "and how alike in their love of nature to Christ's love of creation, or with the reverence toward nature by the Saint from Assisi!"

Nonni in Japan

"Everything is a way to God," explained a young Buddhist monk after he had spent another night in the open air. "The closer we get to things, the closer we get to Him."

"If we look at those things correctly, and if we use them adequately," I added, and the pious Asian monk agreed with me.

In Japan, almost every bloom has its own festival, with the cherry blossom festival being the most celebrated. When on that day guests come to visit, the children welcome them joyfully, offering them all kinds of sweets on pretty little plates. For this ceremony the children are beautifully dressed and decorated, looking like colorful butterflies moving with lively ease. There is really nothing more lovely and graceful than these little Japanese girls: they take part in all Japanese festivals.

In January, there is the New Year holiday where the fire brigade demonstrates its tricks.

In February, there is the Plum-Blossom Viewing, prepared far in advance and celebrated by the entire people.

In March, the famous Girls' Day (Hina Matsuri) is celebrated. In the preceding weeks, most unusual dolls are offered at many sales booths. The Girls' Day is a big children's festival, during which the little ones are honored and celebrated in every imaginable way.

In April is the Cherry Blossom Festival: Thousands of people walk under the blossoming trees, enjoying the magic of that splendor.

In May, the Boys' Day is celebrated. – In June, the Rice Day. – In July, the Day of the Stars. – In August, the Day of Country Dance. – In September, the Festival of the Moon. – In October, the Mushroom Festival. – In November, the Chrysanthemum Festival and in December the second Rice Festival.

Nonni in Japan

CHAPTER 27
I Am Guided to the Japanese Theater

Quickly I got ready and left the room with my visitor. Soon we were in the car that was waiting for us. It drove off through the streets with great speed as it is customary in Tokyo.

To break the silence, I asked: "How did you hear that I had come to Japan?"

"I have read about it in the papers," he replied. "I knew it would be a great joy for our Japanese children if you visited them."

After a short while the car stopped.

"Here we are," said the Japanese gentleman, getting out and helping me out, too. We were standing in front of a big building.

"Is this the theater in which your many young friends have gathered?" I asked my guide.

"Yes, this is the theater. Over a thousand children are waiting!" he replied, leading me to a relatively small door.

"Why such a small entrance for such a huge building?" I asked.

He answered: "We got off at the back of the theater. This is a private entrance only. I have chosen it so that we can get into the building unseen."

Aha… the mystery begins, I thought to myself.

My guide led me to the small door, and we entered the big building.

First, we went through a corridor. At the end there was a second door. My guide opened it and asked me to follow him.

When I had gone through, I hesitated, as we found ourselves in a big room. The strange thing, however, was that this room was completely empty. At the other end was a huge theater stage, yet the mighty purple curtain was rolled down. There were countless chairs on the floor in long rows, from wall to wall.

I was puzzled. Despite the emptiness of the room, I could hear the humming of thousands of happy children's voices. I stood still to listen more carefully. I turned to my Japanese guide and asked: "Where are all these children I hear?"

"They are upstairs above our heads, waiting for the performance."

Meanwhile we walked a good stretch towards the theater stage. My guide stopped and said: "You have seen the theater stage. Now, have a look at the auditorium."

What did we see? In the rear of the theater hall were seemingly endless rows of children – from the bottom to the ceiling. They were far away, and therefore, appeared very small.

"Who are these children?" I asked my guide.

"They are those whom we are entertaining here today," he replied. "The whole

Nonni in Japan

auditorium in the rear has been reserved for them. There are more than one thousand happy children."

My Japanese friend guided me through a door into a small room from which a few steps led up to the stage. As the curtain was down, the children in the rear of the hall could not see us.

In the middle of the stage was a huge armchair. My guide said: "Now we can begin."

I looked at him questioningly.

He then informed me: "The first act of your performance is that you sit calmly on that chair, remaining still and quiet for about five minutes."

Now the light dawned on me, and I began playing my role.

Nonni in Japan

Nonni in Japan

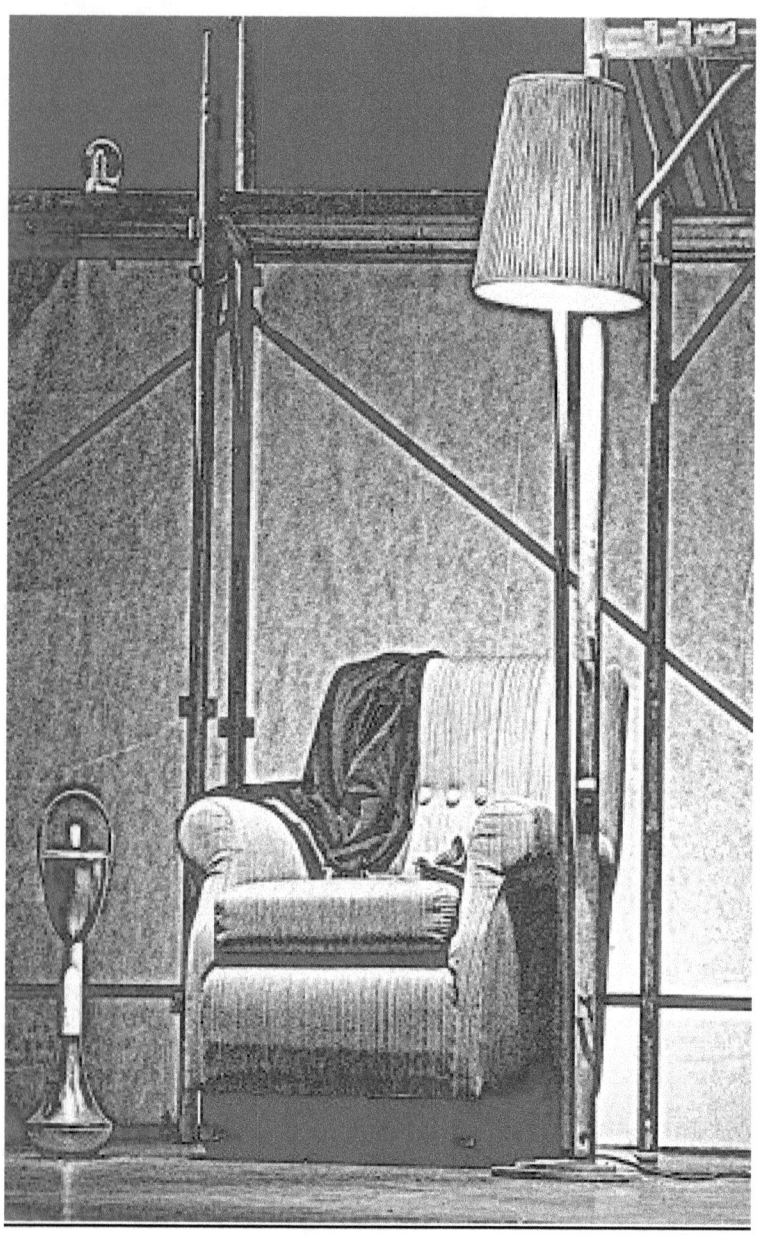

Nonni in Japan

CHAPTER 28
I Play a Role on Stage in the Japanese Theater

With a smile I sat down in the big armchair. Then my Japanese friend said: "If you will, please, remain seated while I step in front of the curtain and give an introduction to the children."

I felt I understood my situation well; therefore, I agreed to follow my Japanese guide's request. I remained seated calmly in the armchair while he stepped in front of the curtain, where the thousand young spectators could see him well. He gave a clear signal with a small bell he held in his hand, and the young audience in the rear stopped chatting.

He shouted with a loud voice – in Japanese, of course:

"My dear children! You are about to see something extraordinary, something totally new and curious. In a moment I shall lift the curtain and you will see a poet in the middle of the stage – a real, living poet who has come to Japan from the other side of the globe! He has come from the island of Iceland, which lies in the Atlantic Ocean. You will see for yourselves that this man looks completely different from us. His hair is not black, but snow white. His skin is not tawny, but pale. He is seated in the middle of the stage. Let us now have a look!"

Then he lifted the curtain slowly, and the surprised children sat in complete silence. I remained in the armchair, silently, as all eyes settled on me. After a few minutes, the curtain rolled down again, slowly and carefully.

My performance must be over, I thought to myself.

However, I was wrong, as my Japanese guide came running towards me quickly.

"That was the first act!" he said with a smile. "Now for the second. I shall tell the children something, and the curtain will be lifted again. As soon as the curtain is raised, I would like you to get up and take a few steps forward. Then, give a little speech to the children, preferably in your mother tongue. We don't want the children thinking we tricked them by placing a mannequin in the armchair! This will prove that you are real!"

I had to give in. I sat down again in the armchair while the guide stepped in front of the curtain a second time and said: "My dear children! You shall not only see the poet who comes from the other side of the world, but now you shall hear him speak in his mother tongue!"

When the children heard this, they became extremely excited and full of anticipation. And then, there was complete silence in the big auditorium. I waited patiently until the curtain went up.

Nonni in Japan

I looked at my auditorium attentively. The children sat there quiet as mice. Again, all eyes were on me. I stood up from my armchair and went forward to the front edge of the stage. There I stopped for a few moments, pondering what I could say to the many children. At the same time I regarded my audience more closely. Never in my life had I felt such an excited and attentive group of youngsters.

Finally, I began to speak slowly, solemnly, and with a loud voice. The young listeners sat in their seats as if spellbound. I knew that nobody understood the least of my speech, so there would be little consequence as far as the content was concerned.

I greeted the children in my mother tongue – the sonorous, beautiful Old Norse language:

"*Mer pàd stör gledi at tala vit ykkur, gòtu og duglegu Japönsku börn!*" ["I am very happy to speak to you, dear good and diligent Japanese children!"]

I also said a few words in other European languages: German, French, Danish… When I had spoken for a few minutes, it occurred to me that the children might be pleased if I closed my speech by the only Japanese words I had learned, which seemed well-fitted for the occasion.

I concluded: "Nippon banzai!" which means: "Long live Japan!"

I had hardly shouted those words when an overwhelming jubilation arose so that one almost went deaf and blind. "Banzai! Banzai!" repeated the children even a long time afterwards in enthusiastic outbursts of cheering.

That storm of enthusiasm ended my first experience at a Japanese theater.

I bowed before the great crowd of my juvenile listeners who now in turn shouted countless "Banzai!" towards me. Then my Japanese guide accompanied me to a small room nearby.

There were several gentlemen and ladies. They welcomed me with the greatest kindness and thanked me for having entertained the children. They even gave me many souvenirs. Soon, however, I had to take leave from them.

Having said Good-bye, one of the gentlemen who spoke German very well guided me outside, called a car and helped me get on.

"I shall take you back to Jochi Daigaku University," he said.

When he noticed that I hesitated in my walking, he said: "It appears you have problems with your leg. May I ask you if I might help somehow?" he added, compassionately.

"I am unsure what you might do," I answered. "For many years, I have suffered from heavy rheumatism which has grown worse and worse, so that I often have strong pains and walk with difficulty."

"If you would allow me to help," continued my companion, "I think I can."

"I will gladly accept any suggestion, with pleasure!" I replied. "What do you have in mind?"

He answered: "First, I will have you see a friend of mine, a highly regarded Japanese physician, who will examine your bad leg. Then, we shall go to an acupuncture practitioner."

"Acupuncture?" I interrupted. "A Chinese doctor who heals with needles?"

"No, no, not to a Chinese doctor, a Japanese acupuncture practitioner", replied my companion.

Nonni in Japan

"I thought acupuncturists practiced in China only. Are there also acupuncturists in Japan?" I asked.

"Yes, Sir, quite a few," he continued. "We have adopted this art from the Chinese."

"I thank you for your offer," I said. "When can we do this?"

"We can do so right now," he said. Thus, the matter was settled, and my companion told the driver where to take us. About half an hour later, the car stopped in front of an imposing building: the Japanese hospital.

Nonni in Japan

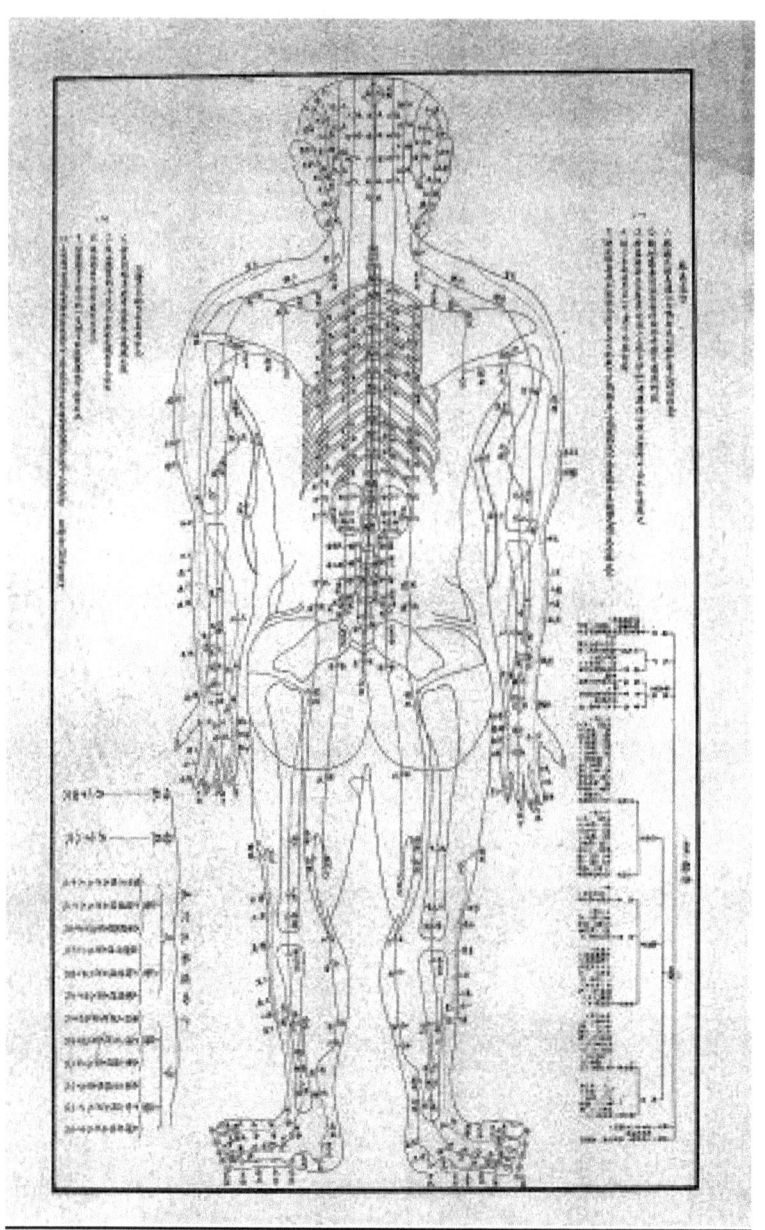

CHAPTER 29
The Acupuncturist with Golden Needles

On entering the big building, the porter guided us into the reception room, where the Japanese physician soon appeared. Luckily, he spoke English as well as my companion, so language was no problem.

When I described how I suffered from rheumatism in my leg, he examined the leg and asked me: "Would you like to be treated by an acupuncturist?"

"I must admit that I don't really know what an acupuncturist is," I responded. "I know of that word, but I have no idea what one does. However, I am willing to do anything you suggest."

"Fine," said the physician. "I recommend you try acupuncture. You will be informed about it shortly, but first, I want to get an x-ray of your bad leg."

Nonni in Japan

He made a signal with a bell. The door was opened and a Japanese boy of about sixteen years came in. The physician took a piece of paper and wrote a few words on it and gave it to the boy. After reading the notice, the boy gave me a signal to follow him.

I glanced at my Japanese guide. He told me in English that I should go with the boy who had been given the order to have my leg photographed by x-rays. So, I got up and left the room with the boy.

My young companion guided me through various corridors. Finally, we arrived in a room with mighty apparatus. He showed me to a lounger, above which was affixed a peculiar technical miracle. It looked like a huge lamp hanging from the ceiling.

I turned to the young guide, pointed with my hand to the mighty construction and asked in English what it was.

Nonni in Japan

Apparently, the boy had understood my question because he answered with the single word: "Röntgen!"

I was relieved because now it was clear that my leg would now be x-rayed.

I reclined in the lounger under the mighty apparatus which began to buzz and roar.

After a short while the young Japanese came back, stopped the roaring machine, and asked me to get up. We walked back to the waiting physician, who asked me to come back the next day. He would tell me then what I had to do.

So, for the time being, I returned to Jochi Daigaku University. The next day I went again to the Japanese physician to hear further suggestions. He received me very kindly, and among other things he told me the following: "The picture taken yesterday shows that complete healing is not possible. Not only is the muscle badly damaged, but the bone as well. However, it will be possible to alleviate pain.

"When you travel back to Europe, I would suggest you show the picture of your bad leg to a physician there and ask for his advice. He might send you to one of the European spas for a treatment. However, while you remain in Japan, I would advise you to seek one of our acupuncturists. They would probably be able to help you best."

"Doctor, is this the treatment accomplished with needles?" I asked.

"Yes, that is the best advice I can give you under these circumstances," he said.

I asked the physician to recommend a competent acupuncturist. The physician answered: "One will visit you tomorrow in Jochi Daigaku University. His treatment is really the best advice I can give you while you are here in Japan."

Nonni in Japan

I knew very little about those peculiar Japanese "healers." I said: "What can you tell me about acupuncture?"

"I will only say to take the advice seriously," answered the physician. "You will soon meet the acupuncturist for yourself, and he will tell you best about his art."

"Can anyone really heal diseases by using golden needles?" I continued.

"Yes, without any doubt, in certain cases, it can be done," replied the friendly physician. "In Japan, many diseases are healed with the help of those needles."

I had another question: "How are the needles used?"

He explained: "They are inserted slowly into the muscle of the ailing joint. This procedure is repeated until finally the healing sets in or until one must admit that the patient cannot be healed."

Nonni in Japan

We talked a bit more about that strange art. In the end, I planned to follow the advice of the Japanese physician. When I had returned to the university I went to my friend, University Director Heuvers, to inform him about my decision and to hear his opinion about the matter.

"I think you should take the advice given by the physician. After all, the art of acupuncture is taken seriously here in Japan, and quite a few patients have been healed by that procedure," he said. He then added, "I myself know a competent acupuncturist personally. If you wish, I can recommend you to him, and ask him to treat you with his golden needles for a few weeks."

I thanked my good friend for this information and advice, and after a few days, my acupuncture treatment began.

How did it go?

Around 10am, there was a knock at my door. I shouted: "Come in!

Nonni in Japan

The door opened and a nice young Japanese entered, approached and made a deep bow. He straightened up quickly and said in good English: "I have been asked to treat you. Is it convenient if I start now?"

"Sure," I answered, "I am ready."

The young man pulled a neat little box out of a leather case and said: "I have heard that you are suffering from rheumatism in one leg."

"Yes, that's correct. Do you think you will succeed healing my leg with your needles?"

The young man looked at me attentively and replied: "Before I can answer your question, I would like to know how old you are."

"I am exactly 80 years old now and have been suffering from rheumatism for more than 40 years."

"If that is the case," he said, "I can only promise you substantial improvement through my treatment. At your age, and after such a long disease, a complete healing is impossible."

"So," I said, "you don't promise me a complete cure, but an improvement of my condition. That's enough. And, if you can keep this promise, I shall be very grateful to you!"

Then, this very strange treatment began. The young acupuncturist took a very long, extremely thin golden needle out of a fine leather case and asked me to lie down on my bed. I did, and waited with great anticipation for what was going to happen,

The young needle doctor placed a chair beside the bed and sat down. He placed a thin silken cloth which he had brought along over the naked bad leg. I prepared to feel great pain when the needle pierced deeply into the muscle. But, although the needle stabbed directly into the muscle of my leg, the pain was very slight, and therefore, easily bearable.

Nonni in Japan

Each treatment lasted about a half an hour, with needles inserted into several spots along the muscles, and later pulled out again. This was sometimes repeated every day, sometimes every other day. Then there would be a pause of a few days, after which the treatment began again. It went on like that for several weeks until the acupuncturist explained me that the treatment was over.

I asked for the bill and paid the very modest fee for which the needle doctor had asked. After a few days he came to see how I was doing. It was a pleasure for me to tell him that I was feeling much better.

During his last visit, he gave me an unexpected surprise.

While sitting and chatting with him in my room, he took a small bundle which he had placed on a chair and opened it, revealing a beautiful, silken Japanese robe. He handed it to me with the following words: "My wife asks you to please accept this small gift as a souvenir from us."

I felt ashamed accepting such a precious gift, which was probably as costly as the fee which he had received from me for treating my bad leg.

However, I had to accept his truly beautiful and precious gift with grace and gratitude.

Nonni in Japan

Nonni in Japan

Nonni in Japan

CHAPTER 30
In the Residential Area of Japanese Youth

One day, director Heuvers came to me and asked: "Would you like to visit our 'Settlement' and tell some stories to the children living there?"

"Your 'Settlement'?" I asked. "What is that?"

"It is a sort of care for the poor," he explained. "Not far from our university, we have rented a few small buildings and furnished them. There, we host poor Japanese children during the day. The aim is to get these children off the street, watch over them and educate them a bit. Their parents are not necessarily Christian, but very grateful because they don't have the time or resources to provide for their children."

I thanked Mr. Heuvers for his invitation. I was very interested in getting to know more, and so I went with a younger inhabitant of the university. To get there, we took one of the many electric streetcars running through the streets of Tokyo.

We reached our destination in about a half hour. This part of the city seemed strange to me. I looked in all directions, then asked, "In which part of Tokyo are we?"

He said: "This is where the poorer inhabitants of Tokyo live."

Indeed, looking closer, one could hardly see anything but endless rows of small, modest, one-story houses.

"All these small houses look like small peas in a pod," I commented

"Yes, you are right," said my friend. "That's how the Japanese want them to be. They insist the houses be small."

"Are they against higher and bigger houses?" I asked.

Nonni in Japan

"I will tell you," my companion began. "Japan is a very volcanic country, with more than one thousand earthquakes per year, big and small. That is a very great danger. Now and then in Japan, whole cities are destroyed by earthquakes, as happened in 1923. Imagine this in a city of several million inhabitants! Because of this danger, the Japanese prefer to build small, low houses in the big cities, in most cases from wood. Although the buildings may be easily destroyed during heavy earthquakes, they are quickly and easily reconstructed afterward."

"That makes sense," I mused.

He added: "Let's assume that tonight this suburb would be completely destroyed by a strong earthquake. In a few weeks everything could be reconstructed as before. How long would it take to rebuild big palaces of stone? The modest Japanese people live happily in their small wooden houses with less fear of destruction."

Nonni in Japan

By now we had reached the 'Settlement.' It was a neat, single-story building surrounded by playgrounds. I looked around nosily, seeing the building and the empty playgrounds – but no trace of any children. I was surprised, for I had been invited to see the children and tell them stories. This location seemed empty!

I turned to my companion and said: "All I see looks very nice, but where are the children?"

"You will see them soon," answered my guide.

We crossed the nearest playground to the entrance of the building. When the door was opened, my companion said: "Now I will introduce our children to you!"

Here I made big eyes! I beheld a lovely, furnished theater hall with a nice stage and an attractive curtain. This auditorium had no chairs or benches. Instead, mats and carpets had been spread on the floor. In Japan, one

Nonni in Japan

does not normally sit on chairs or benches. That goes well with the small houses and with the Japanese love of nature.

The children took their seats on the floor, smiling at us happily as we entered the crowded room. After we sat down, our cozy social get-together began. We would be there several hours. One surprise followed the next in our conversation! I have seldom seen such a big meeting of boys and girls who were so happy and cheerful and spontaneous all the time as was this small group of Japanese children!

At the start, I asked my companion: "Who oversees the children here?"

"There are a few people of Jochi Daigaku University who check if everything is ok," he replied. "However, the Japanese children also know how to keep order and calm among themselves."

Then he said: "By now, everybody knows that you wish to tell them a story."

Nonni in Japan

"When do you think I should begin?"

"I think it would be best if you start right now. Later, the children will take care of entertainment... you will see!"

A signal was given and there was absolute silence. My guide got up and said a few words in Japanese to the audience, then whispered in German that I had been introduced and the story could now begin. I got up, with my interpreter only a few steps away to translate my story, sentence by sentence.

It must have been interesting for my young listeners to see such a strange man with such foreign speech! When I finished, they thanked me by clapping their hands vigorously. Then, it was their turn: the quick and small children took over as entertainers with astonishing proficiency.

In my mind's eye I can still see clearly the image of that audience. The whole floor of the settlement theater was covered with

Nonni in Japan

mats and carpets arranged according to the age of the children. The youngest were in one area; they did not perform, but regarded everything attentively and listened carefully. The older boys and girls formed groups and sections, too, and were among those who performed now and then. The older boys told exciting stories from the stage; the older girls showcased splendid dances.

I can still see all that so clearly as if it was going on in this moment! I remember vividly how the older boys were asked who might narrate another short story. The boys looked at each other, pondering a few moments…then, one of them decided to go ahead. He might have been about twelve years old. Leaping forward quickly, reached the stage, and without any shyness or bewilderment, the Japanese boy began to tell his story. I was amazed by the confidence with which this twelve-year old narrated continuously for about a quarter of an hour, and how he emphasized his story by very natural gestures. When he returned to his seat, it was the turn of a girl of his age to perform one of the most splendid Japanese dances. Thus, the afternoon passed in the most pleasant way.

You will recall how I have long admired and loved the Japanese history and culture. At the end of the children's performance, some words of the apostle of Japan came to my mind:

"The Japanese are the most intelligent people I have come to know. They are the desire of my heart and the delight of my soul."

Throughout their performances, I marveled that these young boys and girls were so self-reliant and how they sat so quietly and calmly without moving as long as a performance lasted or as long as a story was told them. The little ones remain seated on crossed legs for hours without changing position even once or moving their bodies restlessly. Thinking how fidgety much older children in other countries are during my lectures, and how difficult it is sometimes to keep them quiet even for only half an hour, I must say that Japanese children are real masters of self-control. I surmised all that would not be possible without the involuntary exercise in the sling on the back of elder siblings or on the back of their mothers. I asked my companion where Japanese children learn that extraordinarily high level of self-control. His answer was: "As soon as the Japanese children are six months old, they have to learn to sit still, even though they might not like it; even if sitting uncomfortably on their still-weak legs is painful."

I wondered: "Is that possible for children of only six months?"

"Here in Japan, it is," was the short answer. "Furthermore, as soon as the six-month-olds can sit, they are taught how to greet others. The child's upper body is bent forward as often as possible to practice bowing correctly and nicely."

"Why is it so important that six-month-old children know how to bow?" I felt compelled to ask further. I, the Northerner, could not understand this.

"In Japan, it is customary that children learn to greet as soon as they can walk. And when they are one year old, they must know exactly whom they must greet, and how to greet them properly," my companion explained tersely. "The worst that could happen to Japanese parents seems to be if their children are criticized for bad manners. That would be an offense against the family's honor and has worse consequences than any other misdemeanor."

Now I was better able to understand the great politeness towards me in the "country of the rising sun." All throughout my life, I have not experienced any other people as polite and courteous as the Japanese.

Nonni in Japan

Nonni in Japan

CHAPTER 31
Unexpected Event in the Imperial University

One day, when I was sitting at my desk, there was an unexpected knock on my door.

I called: "Come in!"

The door opened and an unknown Japanese gentleman came in.

"Am I not disturbing?" he asked as he approached.

"Not at all," was my reply, and I offered him a chair.

He introduced himself as a professor at the Imperial University of Tokyo. His name sounded typically Japanese, and, unfortunately, the unusual nature of that language prevents me from remembering how to pronounce it.

He continued: "Professor Ichikawa has asked me to give you his best regards…"

I hesitated when I heard those words. Professor Ichikawa? Was he known to me?

"Ichikawa teaches English language and literature, as well as languages from which the present English language derives, especially the Old Norse language spoken on the island of Iceland."

"Yes!" I exclaimed, with faint recollection. "Here in Tokyo, my mother tongue is taught!"

"Surely, yes," said my visitor with a smile. "Professor Ichikawa teaches Icelandic language and literature at the Imperial University. For, those wishing to study English on a scientific basis must also study Icelandic, as the English language is derived in such large part from the Icelandic language."

It was still a great surprise that my dear Icelandic mother tongue was being taught to Japanese students by a Japanese professor right here in Tokyo!

Nonni in Japan

My visitor continued: "When Professor Ichikawa learnt that you, a true Icelander and Icelandic storyteller, were visiting and staying in Tokyo, he had the idea to invite you to one of his lectures about the Icelandic language and literature."

It was a pleasure to accept this invitation honoring me and my homeland, and we fixed the day and hour on the spot. My visitor assured me that Professor Ichikawa would send another professor of the Imperial University to pick me up by car, and then take me home afterward.

On the day of my visit, I was thusly escorted a rather long way through the city and up to the Imperial University. When we arrived, I made big eyes, as the University was situated in a most beautiful spot in the middle of the city. The entire campus seemed like a wondrous garden, with the grounds covered by splendid palaces – all belonging exclusively to the university. When I saw this splendor, I thought of the fairytale palaces in the wonderful stories from "A Thousand and One Nights" which I had read in my youth.

We drove up in front of one of the bigger university palaces. I asked my companion: "What is this beautiful building used for?" He replied: "This is the library of the Imperial University. It was built by Mr. Rockefeller, one of the richest persons of the United States of America, who donated it to the university."

The car went a little further and stopped again in front of another splendid building. We got off there and entered the magnificent edifice where Professor Ichikawa lectured on the Old Norse language and literature.

My companion led me to the hall where Professor Ichikawa received us with the greatest courtesy. His students were many young Japanese men who endeavored to

Nonni in Japan

learn my mother tongue, Old Norse, in which the Edda, the sagas and skaldic poetry had been written.

When I had greeted them, they returned my greeting by quoting Old Norse texts from the Edda and the sagas for my enjoyment. It was very interesting for me to hear how giftedly these Japanese students read, pronounced, and translated my mother tongue. It was, of course, not easy for them, and I had to admire their amazing efficiency. What the students quoted was the famous piece from the Old Norse mythology called "Thor's journey to Utgardaloki".

Professor Ichikawa then turned and asked if I would please read the corresponding piece loudly and slowly in the Old Norse language so that the Japanese students could listen to an authentic pronunciation. That was an easy task for me!

We passed a few hours reading and translating together, and then the professor invited me to refreshments with him and the students. We remained together for another very pleasant hour, chatting and enjoying the world-famous Japanese tea ceremony. I have forgotten some details of our conversation, but I know I expressed my amazement with and admiration of the enthusiasm and interest with which the Japanese studied the Old Norse language. In reply, they said: "Does the wonderful Old Norse literature not deserve such interest? Do its roots not also reach us in the country of the rising sun? Scholars call those connections the 'Indo-Germanic Language Family,' referring to similarities between the east and the north. This is among the most beautiful literature in the whole world. Surely the well-educated people in Europe think so, too?"

"Yes," I answered, "and yet, Old Norse is only the mother tongue of a very small people on the island of Iceland. It is rather difficult to learn that language. Therefore,

Nonni in Japan

Old Norse literature does not hold the prominence today that you might think. Few others disseminate this literature as much as in Germany, but it is still highly esteemed there."

Professor Ichikawa agreed, adding that the Old Norse literature fully deserved that recognition. We sat together for a long time discussing the merits of Old Norse language and literature.

These Japanese students astonished me by the progress they made in their studies. I asked if it was difficult, given the extremely great difference between Japanese and the Old Norse language, and the completely different ways of thinking of both peoples. One student gave me an answer typical of the Japanese: "One has to admit that it is difficult to study that language; but we love its beauty and its greatness. With diligence and perseverance, difficulty can be conquered soon enough." I recalled

Director Heuvers saying I would hardly find a more diligent people than the Japanese in the whole world.

As we were chatting, we heard the car signal from outside that it was time to end the session. I had to take leave of dear Professor Ichikawa and his competent students and return to Jochi Daigaku University.

Nonni in Japan

Nonni in Japan

CHAPTER 32
I Give a Lecture at "L'Étoile du Matin"

During my time in Tokyo, I received countless invitations to give lectures – especially in schools and other educational establishments in the capital.

One day, a Japanese gentleman in European attire came in and greeted me. "Bonjour, Monsieur!" he said, and asked: "Will you please allow me to talk with you for a few moments?"

He sat down at my invitation, and continued: "I have come to ask you if you are willing to come to 'L'Étoile du Matin' (*that is, the educational establishment called* The Morning Star) in Tokyo and give a lecture to our Japanese students and their teachers?"

"It would be my pleasure," I replied. "I hope you will permit me to ask a few questions about the establishment, since this is the first time I have heard of it."

"Of course, of course! I shall try and answer them all."

"It has a French name, '*L'Étoile du Matin*'. Is it a Japanese or French establishment?"

"It is a purely Japanese college. Its name is French because it was founded by a French society which still runs it."

"Which society is this?"

"The Missionaries of the Society of Mary, the Montfortan Padres, founded by Louis Grignion de Montfort, the great reformer of religious life in France and founder of the order."

"Do you belong to that society yourself?"

"Yes, I do".

"How many pupils are there in *L'Étoile du Matin*?"

"There are one thousand four hundred students at the moment."

Nonni in Japan

"Fourteen hundred students! This must be one of the biggest educational establishments of Tokyo!"

"Yes, presumably so."

"Which language do your pupils and students speak?"

"All of them speak Japanese, of course, because they were born in Japan. But many of them also understand and speak French. And those will be your audience."

"May I thus give my lecture in French?"

"Yes, you can. And you will be understood by all of them without any difficulty."

"That is settled then. I shall give the lecture with pleasure!" The date was fixed on one of the following days, and when the occasion arrived, I was picked up by one of the professors of *L'Étoile du Matin*.

After a rather long drive through the streets of the Japanese capital, we reached a section with a small garden city. Our car stopped in front of a mighty entrance.

A porter received us and invited us to enter.

I had a look around but could not see a school! What I saw resembled more a small town than an educational establishment. I asked my companion: "Where is *L'Étoile du Matin*? I thought it should be around here."

My companion replied: "Actually, *L'Étoile du Matin* consists of all these buildings." It seemed to me a veritable labyrinth of streets and alleys, with many big and small buildings of all sorts.

We encountered a number of Japanese youths, each carrying a camera. Every time I passed one of those photographers, I saw him point the apparatus towards me as it emitted its strange sound. My companion smiled and said: "It is our custom to take pictures of rare visitors."

Nonni in Japan

The further we got, the bigger and nicer were the buildings. Finally, we arrived at a splendid house where I was received by the rector with the greatest courtesy.

"We are very grateful for your coming," he said, "and we are especially pleased that you are going to give us a lecture in French. All our French-speaking pupils are eager to see and hear a man from the north."

As we talked, the hall where I was to give the lecture began to fill.

"All who understand French will be here," said the rector. "There will also be a number of pupils who come out of curiosity, even if they do not understand the language yet. But you will be content with your audience because they will follow your lecture with the greatest attention."

By now the big hall was full.

One of the Japanese professors, Professor Shichida, led me into the hall. On one end of the hall there was a splendid stage to which I was guided.

Before I could start, I was asked sit down while students sang the school hymn accompanied by many musical instruments. I was amazed how beautiful it was and how well it was presented. When that concluded, one of the pupils got up and read a greeting in French. I was not prepared for that… but I was even more surprised when, after his speech, the young Japanese boy came over to me and handed me the text which he had read.

That speech was so delightful that I wish to print it here. For those readers who do not know French, a translation into English will follow:

"Révérend Père,

Nous vous remercions vivement de votre bienveillance d'une si amiable visite par laquelle vous avez bien voulu nous honorer et nous faire plaisir.

Nonni in Japan

Votre nom nous n'était pas inconnu. Quelques unes de vos œuvres sont déjà traduites en japonais. Nous croyons y rencontrer des scènes pathétiques prises sur le vif, des passages si riches de cœur et de poésie, des paroles vibrantes d'émotion, des yeux imprégnés de tristesse, des regards chargés de reconnaissance, des physiognomies empreintes d'une profonde terreur, des âmes émues par les plus vifs sentiments de foi et de sympathie. Tout cela nous émeut et nous édifie.

Votre séjour au Japon vous a encore mis en contact de plus en plus intime avec le people japonais, surtout avec les jeunes japonais, et vous avez déclaré maintes fois que vous aimiez le Japon profondément et que vous étiez un grand ami des enfants japonais.

Nous croyons répondre à votre sympathie en nous efforçant de nous conformer advantage aux règlements de l'école ainsi qu'aux principes d'une vie exemplaire. Le zèle que nous avons pour remplir nos devoirs est d'autant plus grand que notre patrie traverse actuellement une de ses heures les plus pénibles dont l'issue échappe encore à tout prévision.

Un eminent talent d'artiste, comme le vôtre, appelé à exercer une grande influence sur les cœurs des enfants de tous les pays, peut bien réaliser un rapprochement international par-dessus les frontiers. C'est le souhait le plus ardent que nous vous adressons aujourd'hui.

Nous vous prions, Révérend Père, d'agreer les témoignages de notre respect ainsi que nos vœux sincères pour votre bonheur et pour le plein succès de votre mission.

Au nom de tous me camarades ici presents

T. Ashida

1re année du lycée."

Nonni in Japan

"Reverend Father!

Heartfelt thanks for your dear visit by which you wanted to honor and please us.

Your name was not unknown to us. Some of your works have already been translated into Japanese. We believe to find in them touching scenes taken from real life, as well as paragraphs rich in heartwarming poetic sentiments, words that vibrate with inner movement, eyes full of deep sadness, looks full of gratitude, faces contorted by the most violent terror, souls moved by the most vivid feelings of faith and love. All this touches us and builds us up.

Your stay in Japan has strengthened your contact with the Japanese people, especially with the Japanese youth. Often you have said that you loved Japan very much and that you were a great friend of the Japanese youth.

We believe that we honor your goodwill by trying to stick to school rules as best we can and to the principles of an exemplary life. Our zeal for the fulfillment of our duties is especially great at the moment because our country is going through one of the most difficult hours of its history whose outcome cannot be predicted at all.

An outstanding artistic talent like yours which is called to exercise an important influence on the hearts of children of all countries will certainly be able to bring about an international approximation even across national frontiers. – This is the ardent wish that we address to you today.

Reverend Father, we ask you to accept our most respectful blessings for your personal luck and complete success of your mission.

In the name of all my classmates who are present

T. Ashida

First year of lyceum"

Nonni in Japan

At this point, it would have been my turn to go to the stage and begin. But I was so touched by this gesture that I was not able to speak! Never in my life had I felt as deep a connection than with these young people in the Far East… none before had seen so clearly the deep sense of my work and the longing of my heart, nor had anybody ever expressed my intentions so convincingly as this young Asian boy. I could only step forward and tell his classmates and teachers that they had understood me correctly and that he had properly interpreted the meaning of my coming and longing to be there.

Nonni in Japan

Nonni in Japan

CHAPTER 33
More Lectures to Japanese Youth

It is true: The Japanese youth exceeded all my expectations, both at the 'Morning Star' college and everywhere I went.

My readers will remember how courteous the little Japanese boy on the steamer "Chichibu Maru" was towards me right from the beginning, how faithfully he stood by my side during the entire voyage from America to Japan, and how he drew my attention to everything that was important and interesting to his young eyes.

I was further amazed by the enthusiasm which I saw in all the Japanese youth of all ages during my stay: at their love of nature, their love of poetry, their love of all that is beautiful and great, and at their reverence towards strangers – especially elderly people. I was most pleased by their love of science and their desire to learn. Japanese youth are

Nonni in Japan

incredibly hardworking, sitting over their schoolwork with amazing perseverance and taking little rest.

The fact is that the Japanese children do have a lot to learn, starting at an early age. It is by far not as easy for Japanese children to learn how to read as it is for children with our familiar alphabet of twenty-six characters, with which they can write and read everything offered by their language – if they are clever. It must be a thousand times more difficult for Japanese youngsters to learn to read. Japanese children have over one thousand two hundred characters to be learned and distinguished from one another before they can write! Children going on to higher education must learn at least four thousand characters. This is very difficult and requires extraordinarily much practice. In the first few days in Japan, I noticed that almost all pupils wear glasses, even the very young ones. But when I had seen how infinitely many and various characters and

Nonni in Japan

pictures the Japanese script has and how much you must concentrate in order to distinguish things from one another, I understood very well that it is extremely eye-straining to deal with it for hours each day.

Japanese script is derived from the Chinese script and uses these characters for the most part. Words are not composed of individual letters as is the case with the script of occidental peoples. On the contrary: here, every word has its own character. Thus, the language has as many characters as words. In fact, Chinese script has about forty-nine thousand characters. Those who want to be a scholar in Japan must know them all and must be able to write them.

Both Japanese and the Chinese scripts run from top to bottom and from right to left. That means, the lines are not arranged horizontally, but vertically, and books do not begin at the front, but at the back. A script would look like this, more or less:

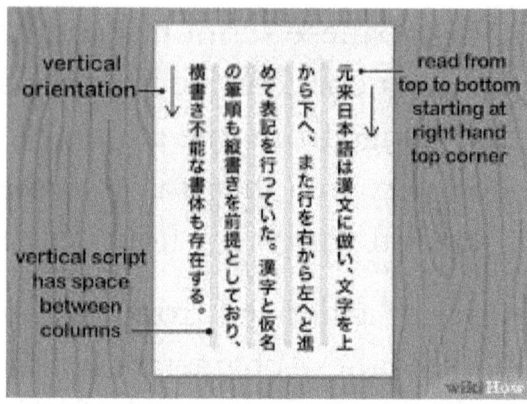

That is quite different from what we are used to at home, and I was always astonished at how fast the Japanese children were able to both read and write. They did so almost as quickly as children with letter-based languages, often even more quickly.

Of course, script and language are rather similar, in that both have many words and glorious laws. Those who know them all are lucky and can clearly make their meanings and desires understood. Those who know less must try to get along with less. Japanese children probably do the same. The teachers told me that around twelve thousand characters have to be learnt and are necessary to get through in life – quite a number of what look like strangely composed pictures, to me, and an understandable answer to the question why so many Japanese children wear glasses.

It is not only reading which asks so much of the Japanese youth; it is also the striving for knowledge, ability, and perfection in work and life. One day, I asked a young university student why Japan asks so much of her youth and why Japanese schools place such high demands on pupils. He answered:

"Japan consists of many isles. On the relatively narrow space of 381,576 square kilometers, there live about eighty-seven million inhabitants… more than half of them in the cities. Only a quarter of the country can be used for agriculture, and mineral resources are too few for the development of sufficient industry. We exert our mental powers to compensate for the lack of material resources."

Nonni in Japan

This explanation satisfied me, and I believe it is correct.

Japanese girls are quite capable. Almost exclusively, their aim is serving their family, so femininity is highly cultivated. Japanese parents strive anxiously to educate their adolescent daughters as maternally as possible. The girls are under very strict control and will be severely punished if they behave in an unwomanly way. In fact, during my time in different cities and villages throughout Japan, I never saw a single negligence in that respect. It is the highest praise for a girl and her parents to be considered feminine. The greatest shame for a girl and her parents would be to call her boyish, and dishonor is the most unbearable fear of Japanese families. Japanese youth know this and live accordingly.

A few days after the touching meeting between the pupils of "L'Étoile du Matin" and me, I received more invitations – some, under somewhat strange circumstances. For instance, I received a letter from the Danish delegation in Tokyo. It read:

"Professor Niels Bohr, an important Danish scholar from Copenhagen, has arrived in Tokyo. This learned gentleman has been invited by the Japanese government because he made an important scientific discovery on the field of atomic theory. His welcoming reception in the Imperial Hotel in Tokyo will be attended by prominent Japanese scholars, as well as several Danish settlers. Your presence is requested as well."

So, of course, I was among the attendees at the big 'Imperial Hotel' where the reception was to take place. I watched as the Danish scholar appeared, followed by a small number of distinguished gentlemen. As soon as he had entered the reception hall, silence fell… but, no long speeches were given, as this was only meant as a first greeting, and the ceremony was soon over.

Nonni in Japan

I thought about leaving the Imperial Hotel and going home, but I was in for my own surprise. All at once, I was surrounded by persons I did not know. They looked at me kindly and they acted like they had something to say to me; however, nobody spoke. I wondered if I should withdraw from them.

Suddenly, two young Japanese women approached me and said in English: "Please excuse us for bothering you. We are teachers at a high school for girls in Tokyo, and we would like to ask you to visit our school and give a lecture to our pupils. We have about six hundred pupils, most of them belonging to the higher social classes."

"You are asking me to give a lecture?" I began. "I shall do so with pleasure! But may I ask in which language? Unfortunately, Japanese is completely foreign to me."

"As our students only speak Japanese," said one of the teachers, "we shall hire an

Nonni in Japan

English interpreter for you. You can give your lecture in English, and the interpreter shall translate everything – sentence by sentence – into Japanese."

"I am happy with that arrangement," I replied. "Now to fix the date and the hour, and have someone pick me up at Jochi Daigaku University."

Both teachers agreed, said goodbye, and left the hall. All the while I was negotiating with the two teachers, the group of young women and men remained in the hall, listening attentively to our conversation.

I silently wondered if they wanted something from me. I turned to those standing nearest to me and asked: "Do you happen to know what those young people are waiting for?"

A young woman answered: "Yes, I do. They have the same request as the two teachers who have just left. The majority are teachers at Japanese high schools and would like to

Nonni in Japan

ask you to give lectures at their schools, too."

"How is it possible that so many people know me?" I wondered.

"Most of them know you from the papers," she answered, "or from one or the other of your books which have been translated into Japanese. These people here have probably read them."

That cleared up this mystery. However, it amazed me that they all had the same idea, on this occasion! There were so many that I needed to write down the names of the schools.

One of the first was "Tonogaota Shudoin." As far as I remember this was a religious house. Also, "Sejio school" was mentioned several times. It was in the middle of Tokyo, they said.

Nonni in Japan

Somebody said: "I know that Madame Ito wants you to give a lecture in her high school."

"What's the name of the school?" I asked.

"Its name is 'Yamato Gakuen'. It lies a bit outside of the city. There are several hundred girls studying there, most of them from distinguished Japanese families."

Then yet another name was mentioned. She, too, wanted to invite me. Her name was Miss Yamamota Watanaba. Her establishment was called "Senno Omori Mikokoro Yochien," and it was situated in "Seibo Bioin." I also heard the name "Hani." This lady was highly praised for founding a big model high school which she also ran herself.

The names of these many Japanese schools were so unusual and difficult that I was hardly able to jot them down correctly. I tried to remember them as best I could.

Nonni in Japan

Each wanted me to tell the Japanese pupils something about Europe or about my life. Such narrations were equally as new and interesting as Europeans feel about what they discover in Asia. I would tell them about my adventures in the Icelandic mountains, my ancestors, the fables and sagas of my homeland, and the cold north with ice and snow.

The attendance at these lectures was always extraordinarily high. The Asian listeners were very interested in hearing of this completely different world, and they always wanted to hear more about it. And why shouldn't I talk about it? It was like creating a bridge from Iceland to Tokyo, from Europe to Asia!

The first of these many engagements was at the prestigious Japanese high school "Yamato Gakuen," which enrolled several hundred Japanese girls. It was situated on the outskirts of the city. Mrs. Ito, the head,

Nonni in Japan

was an extremely educated and proficient lady.

I was picked up from Jochi Daigaku University and driven the long way there.

Arriving at the stately institution, I was surprised that nobody was there to receive me. However, there stood a chair in front of the building. Being a little tired, I sat down and waited. I had only sat there for a few moments when around twenty schoolgirls jumped out of the house. They wore very pretty school uniforms which looked oddly European. They recognized me at once and jumped towards me with a smile. In an instant, they had surrounded me! Those next to me knelt to greet me with a kind smile. Most of the others remained standing upright. All of them, however, looked at me with friendly faces.

It did not take long before I heard that strange metallic sound of a camera nearby. The merriment of the children increased

Nonni in Japan

because they noticed that we were all being photographed together.

Soon afterwards Mrs. Ito stepped out of the house.

I got up, approached the distinguished lady, and greeted her. A few young ladies accompanied Mrs. Ito, presumedly teachers of that establishment. As most of them spoke English, we were able to understand each other without any problems.

Mrs. Ito was courtesy and kindness itself. She excused herself for not being present at my arrival. It seemed, however, that my reception had been planned that way by the students, who were hoping to get my photograph first! The plot succeeded; a few days later, I received a photo in the mail of myself surrounded by this bevy of Japanese girls.

After my lecture, I lingered a few more hours in that splendid institution before I was driven back home.

Nonni in Japan

The invitations to lectures in middle and high schools piled up considerably. I accepted them with pleasure because, they allowed me to learn a lot, and, I pray, do a lot of good.

Nonni in Japan

CHAPTER 34
Visit to and Lecture at Mrs. Hani's Giyu School

Shortly after my visit to Mrs. Ito's school, a Japanese gentleman visited my room in Jochi Daigaku University.

He said: "I have come to ask you if you are willing to pay a visit to Mrs. Hani's Giyu School. The school is situated in the town of Minawisawa, near Tokyo."

"I accept your invitation with pleasure!" I replied. "May I ask what kind of school it is?"

The gentleman said: "Mrs. Hani's Giyu School is one of the most distinguished schools in Japan. Mrs. Hani is quite accomplished, and her school has an excellent reputation. She has great success with her teaching program. There are more than six hundred pupils – boys and girls, all Japanese. However, Mrs. Hani has visited the finest schools in Europe to get to know

Nonni in Japan

their aims and methods, which she has brought back with her. There is hardly a better school in all of Japan."

"What special technique does she use?" I asked my visitor.

"It is difficult to explain because Mrs. Hani's school is unique in many respects. For instance, the tasks which servants carry out in other schools are performed by Mrs. Hani's pupils themselves. Students are responsible for cooking and cleaning."

My interest in Mrs. Hani's ways grew considerably. "If pupils have the added tasks of performing chores, do their lessons and the studies suffer?"

"One might think so," he replied. "But strangely enough, that is not the case. Mrs. Hani's school has a top reputation academically, particularly in scientific education."

Nonni in Japan

I thanked my visitor for the information and promised to visit this renowned school.

On the appointed day, I was driven to Mrs. Hani's "Giyu-Gakuen" - together with Director Heuvers, who had kindly offered to be my interpreter. This time I was to give my lecture in German, as the girls had requested that. Director Heuvers would translate my words, sentence by sentence, into Japanese.

Mrs. Hani received us with the greatest courtesy at the entrance of her school and led us first to a room where some refreshments were being offered.

There, we met two young Japanese ladies who belonged to Giyu-School. I had seen them at the reception of the Danish professor Bohr in the Imperial Hotel. One was Miss Funao, the other one Miss Tachi. They had mentioned this school and expressed their hope I would lecture here. While talking more with these two ladies now, I learned they had once visited Denmark in the small town of Ollerup to study the Swedish-Danish health gymnastics in-depth, hoping to introduce these techniques here. The two ladies were even able to speak with me a little in Danish. They also told me that in Ollerup they had met a few Icelanders – i.e., some of my fellow citizens – and even made friends with them. They mentioned the names "Sigga" and "Gisli" with whom they were still in contact by mail.

While I was talking to Miss Funao and Miss Tachi, director Heuvers chatted with Mrs. Hani. The agenda was set: All pupils, boys and girls, were on their way to the auditorium. When the hall was filled, we would go the stage and begin the lecture from there.

So, we went there at once. As we found the hall completely occupied, I intended to start my lecture right away. Yet, Mrs. Hani had

Nonni in Japan

prepared a wonderful surprise for us: The audience erupted into an extremely beautiful, powerful Japanese song, to our astonishment and delight. The entire audience was singing!

When their song was over, I began the lecture. It lasted a good hour. The procedure was as follows: I spoke a few sentences in German, then university director Heuvers repeated them in Japanese. We continued this way through the entire lecture. Afterward, Mrs. Hani gave us a tour of the sights inside and outside the school. We both said we'd hardly ever seen such a beautiful and functionally equipped school. Along the way, Mrs. Hani told us about her experiences in Paris and other big European cities where she gathered ideas.

After we had seen and admired everything, Mrs. Hani brought us into the dining hall, where lunch had been prepared and all pupils were waiting. We were seated at the

Nonni in Japan

table of honor with Mrs. Hani and a few professors and teachers.

Across from us at our head table were seated a good number of Japanese boys. I was curious to see how these children would behave at the table. These little boys — between eight and ten years approximately — behaved perfectly. I was very surprised they even used knives and forks exactly like Europeans.

After lunch, the housemother showed us even more parts of this fine establishment. Everything was clean and extremely well-equipped. Around the house was a huge garden with many flowers and lovely lawns. The garden had been laid out and tended by the schoolgirls.

We were sorry to have to leave this beautiful place and our extraordinarily proficient hostess Mrs. Hani. These memories are dedicated to her and her exemplary school.

Nonni in Japan

Nonni in Japan

CHAPTER 35
I Am Forced to Give a "Japanese Lecture"

After my visits to the beautiful educational establishments of Mrs. Ito and Mrs. Hani, I received numerous more invitations. The first such came from an establishment for girls situated near our university. That school had been founded by English nuns and was still run by them. Since teachers were Englishwomen, English was used throughout the school as colloquial language, and the invitation stated that I could give my lecture to the Japanese girls in English.

I accepted the engagement, and, on the fixed day, I was driven to the school by car. I gave my speech to a few hundred schoolgirls. Everything went well because all listeners understood the English speech without any problems.

Nonni in Japan

At the end of the lecture, I got a very rare surprise. A Japanese girl asked to speak. I nodded to her. She got up and said in good English: "You have given us a nice lecture in English, thank you very much. But now we have a small wish which you will surely not refuse us: we would like to ask you to say something in Japanese, our native language."

All the girls clapped their hands enthusiastically to show that the wish was also theirs.

I was very surprised by this unexpected request!

Taken aback, I first pondered a few moments what I should answer. The Japanese language is extremely difficult for Europeans, and it still felt completely foreign to me. I could not even have said a single sentence in Japanese. There was a certain pause, while I stood, embarrassed. At last, I gave the following answer:

Nonni in Japan

"You want me to say something in Japanese. But my dear child, how could I do something like that? Up to now I have learned only three Japanese words. More than that? I don't know!"

The clever Japanese girl replied:

"Oh, please, tell us those three words! It's those three words which we would like to hear. It will be a short Japanese speech of three words!"

It could not be helped: I had to come out with my three Japanese words. My young audience was waiting for them with great excitement.

Well... I thought, *why not give them that little joy?*

"Well, dear children, since you are so eagerly asking for it, I shall tell you the three Japanese words which I have learned so far."

In their silence, I began:

Nonni in Japan

"The first Japanese word I learned is 'arigato'."

Roaring applause rang out through the hall! All children clapped their hands enthusiastically.

That was the first point of the Japanese lecture which had been forced upon me.

Now again, silence fell…the second point was to follow.

In a loud, solemn voice, I said: "My second Japanese word is 'Sayonara'!"

Again, roaring applause in the whole hall!

Now the third point – or, rather, the third word. However, when I was about to say that word, it suddenly slipped my mind! What was I going to do?

The entire audience was waiting excitedly…. Oh, what was I going to do?

Nonni in Japan

I searched and searched my memory but could not find the expression. I only knew that it meant "Good evening!"

Defeated, I turned to the audience and said:

"Dear children, the third word is a very difficult word which I cannot recall at the moment. With this term I wanted to wish you a good evening."

"*Kumban wah!*" cried the children immediately, clapping their hands frenetically.

Ah, yes. The third word had been found and my "talk" in Japanese was over. "*Arigato – Sayonara – Kumban wah*" – in English, "Thank you – Goodbye – Good evening." This was sufficient to please the dear Japanese children. They enjoyed this speech very much and gladly forgave me my bad memory.

Nonni in Japan

Nonni in Japan

CHAPTER 36
A Japanese Hans Christian Andersen

One day, Director Heuvers came to my room and invited me to go for a walk with him. He wanted me to meet not only children during my time in Japan, but adults, too.

"Where shall we go? Are we going to visit somebody?" I asked him.

"Yes," he said. "I want you to meet a Japanese gentleman, and I am sure you will enjoy his company."

Quickly I got ready, and after a few minutes, we left the house.

When we were on the street, the director elaborated: "The gentleman whom we are going to visit is Mr. Kishibe, a famous man her ein Japan. He is considered to be the most important narrator of fairy tales in Japan nowadays. He has also written books which are highly esteemed. Mr. Kishibe is fascinated by the great Danish storyteller Hans Christian Andersen, whom you know is considered the greatest narrator of literary fairy tales. He has even made the trip from Japan to Europe to trace the footsteps of Hans Christian Andersen!"

"Did this Mr. Kishibe really travel from Tokyo to Denmark?" I asked.

"Yes, indeed. He went from here to Denmark to see the house in Odense, on the Danish island of Funen (Fyn) where Andersen was born. Mr. Kishibe also wanted to see the surroundings in which he wrote his fairy tales… but when he arrived, he Andersen's birthplace in poor condition. Mr. Kishibe got into contact with the Danish government and convinced them to put Hans Christian Andersen's birthplace under the protection of the state. But back here, Mr. Kishibe has become famous as a fairy-tale poet and fairy-tale narrator in his

Nonni in Japan

own right. By radio he is in contact with the Japanese youth."

After a pause, Mr. Heuvers continued, "Mr. Kishibe also knows the Nonni books. He wishes to be introduced to you."

Hearing all that interesting background, my interest in Mr. Kishibe, the famous Japanese fairy-tale poet and narrator, grew immensely.

Soon, we reached Mr. Kishibe's house.

He received us with the greatest courtesy and we chatted for quite some time in his reception room. As the conversation was in Japanese, I was not able to partake, unfortunately.

From then on, I met Mr. Kishibe many times during my stay in Japan, because the amiable gentleman was an eager friend. He not only gave me all his books and other souvenirs, but – what I liked best - also a shellac record of a story which he himself had recorded. Thus, I could hear his voice whenever I wanted to – I only had to put the record on the player.

One day, he invited me to a festive meal in one of the better hotels of the city. Some distinguished Japanese gentlemen were invited, too. On that occasion, he wanted to show me how such a meal is celebrated in Japan.

We were ushered into a nice room reserved only for us. From the beginning to the end, everything went strictly according to Japanese custom. There were neither chairs nor tables. Each guest received a beautiful Japanese cushion and a small mat. The mat was placed on the floor. The cushion was put on the mat. Each guest sat down on the cushion with crossed legs, in a peculiar position. That was East Asian custom. Despite my best efforts, however, it was absolutely impossible for me to imitate that posture. So, just for me, they put a lot of cushions on top of each other. I still found

Nonni in Japan

it rather difficult, but I managed to perch atop the pile.

Now, followed a typical Japanese meal - a very interesting event for me.

The servants were two extremely polite young Japanese girls. The dishes and the drinks were brought individually to each guest in turn. Every time when the servants came in or went out, they knelt on the floor, greeting the guests by a deep bow. During the meal, the mood was extraordinarily cheerful, from beginning to end. Beside each guest, there were small glasses which were filled by the servants as requested and/or needed. When the meal was over, the guests remained together for quite some time, chatting happily.

Meanwhile, some other visitors entered our small dining-room. They wanted to speak with the famous Mr. Kishibe. This happened in the following way:

Nonni in Japan

Mr. Kishibe got up and knelt on the floor across from the visitor, who was kneeling on the floor, too. In that position, they talked to each other. During their conversation they touched the floor with their foreheads now and then very seriously. The conversation lasted about a quarter of an hour. Then the two gentlemen got up and the visitors took leave from us.

When the visitors left, the feast ended. Now standing, we still talked together for a short time, then we left the hotel. After thanking Mr. Kishibe heartily for such a pleasant event, we said goodbye to each other. Then we got into our car and returned home.

Nonni in Japan

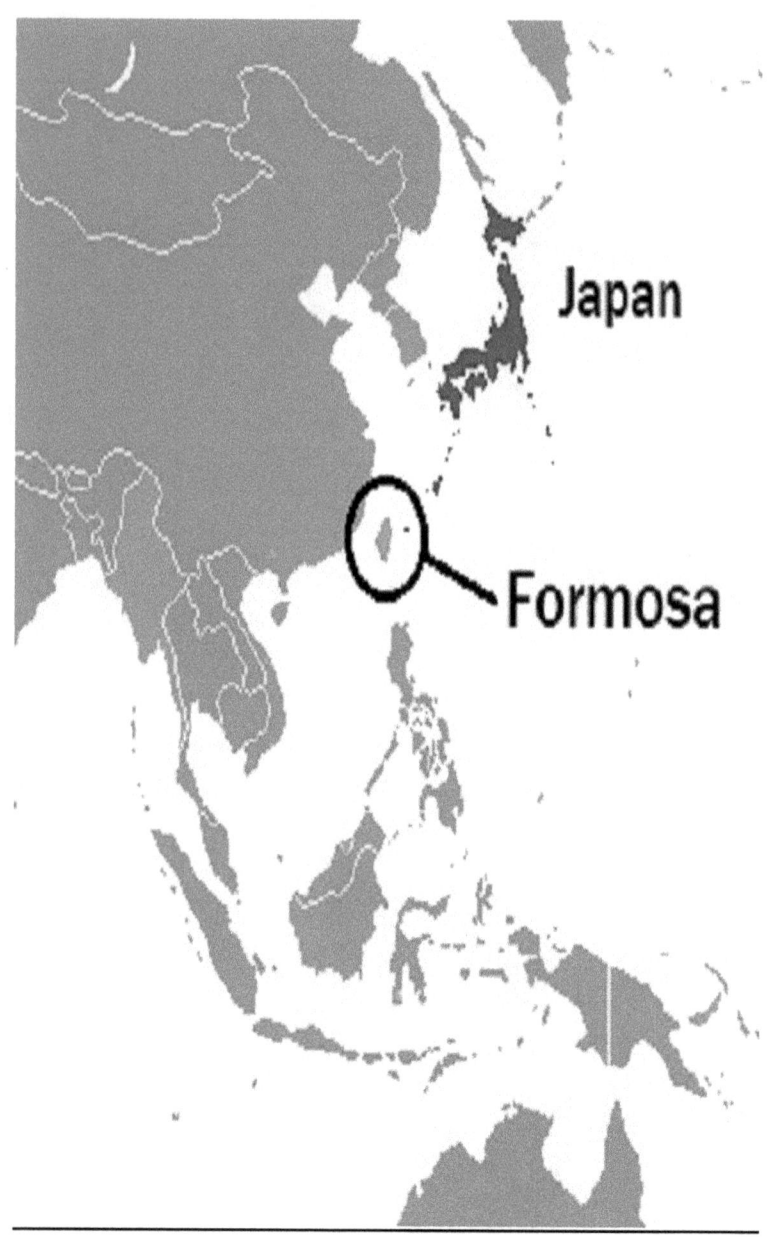

CHAPTER 37
A Short Radio Speech to all Children in Japan

A few days later, Director Heuvers came to me again.

"I would like to ask you a favor," he began. "And I hope you will not turn it down.

"How can I turn down a wish from you?" I asked, smiling.

"What I ask is not really an idea of mine, but Mr. Kishibe's. As you know, he is in frequent contact with the Japanese youth."

I interrupted: "How does he stay in contact with them, scattered all over such a huge country?"

"He does so over the radio, broadcasting to the entire country," was his answer. "By radio, Mr. Kishibe can speak to children all over Japan, and on Formosa Island, as often as he likes. In this way, he gives lectures and narrates fairy tales and uncountable other stories to the children."

He continued: "Mr. Kishibe wants you, too, to give a short speech to the youth via a radio broadcast."

"Of course, it will be a great pleasure for me!" I replied.

My answer was relayed to Mr. Kishibe by telephone. He was very grateful and said he would pick me up soon. And indeed, shortly afterwards Mr. Kishibe arrived at Jochi Daigaku University to bring me to the radio station.

On our way, I asked if there was any special wish concerning my short speech to the Japanese children.

"No," he replied. "You need only greet the children with a few words and introduce yourself. If you wish, you can admonish the children to be good. This is what Japanese children expect from you: in fact, they

Nonni in Japan

expect that from every storyteller; for they don't regard the poet as a mere good-humored entertainer, but also as a guide for good living. Japanese children want to learn, always learn. They will be very eager to hear you speak, because they have heard about you by means of the Japanese newspapers, which have praised you as 'Europe's second Andersen' or as 'Europe's Marc Twain'."

I thanked Mr. Kishibe for his good advice and promised to speak accordingly.

Soon we reached our destination. We got out of the car and went into the studios.

Mr. Kishibe showed me to the microphone which would record my speech. When the time for his broadcast arrived, he first greeted the children in Japanese, then he introduced me and handed me the apparatus. I remembered to keep my speech short. However, I would need an interpreter, as the children only understood Japanese! This was already arranged, as we

Nonni in Japan

had engaged an interpreter in advance. He was a Japanese student who spoke German very well, so I would deliver my speech in German.

Now it was time. I spoke slowly, sentence by sentence. The interpreter repeated what I said in Japanese. Everything went well. The children in Japan and on Formosa Island heard my words in their native language.

I shall repeat it here for my English readers:

"Dear children!

I only want to say a few words to you. My whole life I have had the wish to visit Japan, your fatherland. For I had read a lot about this beautiful country and about her chivalrous inhabitants. Finally, that wish has come true: I have come to Japan, and I am very happy about it!

And now, I want to express a wish: I wish you all, dear children of Japan, to be like your fathers; that one day, you will become worthy of your fathers by doing your duty, by loyalty and chivalry, as well as by reverence and love for your emperor and for your fatherland!"

Nonni in Japan

CHAPTER 38
Speaking to Children in a Japanese Theater

A short time after my radio speech, one of the university professors visited me and asked: "Have you heard about the big feast which will take place in a few days not far from here?"

"No, I have not heard anything about it," I said. "Should I have?"

"Yes," he said. "It seems that you will be invited to tell a few stories to the children. I don't know any details beyond what I have heard." And then, he told me the following:

"It is held in one of the bigger theaters of Tokyo, called 'House of the Avions.' A play will start the festivities. Afterwards, Mr. Kishibe will give a speech. Then, you shall tell a story which will be translated by an interpreter. That's what I've heard."

"Thank you very much for this information," I said. "Is this an event for adults or for children?"

"The program is meant for both. There will be many families with their children. The theater will be booked out."

It did not take long to hear more of this grand event. Mr. Kishibe had a major role in this feast at the 'House of Avions,' but he did not miss out on a single chance to make me happy. He made sure to include me with an express request to tell an exciting story to the audience there. I was glad to accept, of course!

On the appointed day, I was picked up and driven to the festival venue.

Mr. Kishibe spoke with incomparable virtuosity. The story he told must have been extraordinarily interesting, as the audience

Nonni in Japan

sat spellbound listening. Strangely, even I was spellbound by the figure and speech of this man. Although I did not understand a single word, the sound of his language and the facial expressions assured me that his story offered to the children something great, something important. One could see the incredible power of his words moving even us, so that we could take part in what moved him! It put me in mind of the birds and fish to whom Francis of Assisi gave a sermon once. I was no better off concerning my knowledge of Japanese, but, like the birds, I understood the narrator nevertheless because he spoke with much love.

When Kishibe had finished his story, we all thanked him with a roaring applause.

Now it was my turn.

It was not easy for me to speak to a big audience after such a performance! But,

Nonni in Japan

with the help of an interpreter, I told the listeners a story from Old Norse-Germanic times. When I was done, two little Japanese girls entered the stage and gave both Mr. Kishibe and me a lovely bouquet of flowers. Then, I left the stage and looked for a seat among the audience, because various other events were about to take place onstage.

As I sat attentively observing the program, I was dragged out of my thoughts by a number of Japanese children who approached me silently and cautiously, encircling me both from the left and from the right. First, they only looked at me questioningly. I noticed that each child carried something in their hands. I could not imagine what it might be but would soon find out. Some conquered their shyness and came near enough that I could see they carried some caramels or similar sweets which they had gotten from their mothers, and wanted to share with me!

Nonni in Japan

Of course, I could not reject these gifts, so I took them and thanked them. I cannot describe how touched I was by this action of the dear little Japanese kids.

As I have said, I have not found any people who love to celebrate feasts as much as the Japanese – or any who organize children's parties so beautifully. Family parties are celebrated in a most lovely way. There are two things which I find noteworthy about Japanese holidays, especially at the New Year: Everybody plays Hanetsuki, and all children fly Tako (kites). Hanetsuki is played by old and young, also by children, mainly by young girls… but even by boys, while carrying their little brother or sister tied to their backs with mother's kimono! It is remarkable how children are carried not only by their mothers, but also by their fathers, by younger siblings and by the elder brothers.

Nonni in Japan

Playing Hanetsuki is very simple. It is a game like Badminton played by two people, hitting a shuttlecock back and forth with a wooden paddle, but without the net separating the players. The shuttlecock is a small, rounded piece with feathers which sails through the air with the ease of a weighted parachute. This game is played in Japan with a real passion. It is said that the longer players can rally the shuttlecock with their paddles without letting it fall to the ground, the better their fortune will be in the New Year!

Nonni in Japan

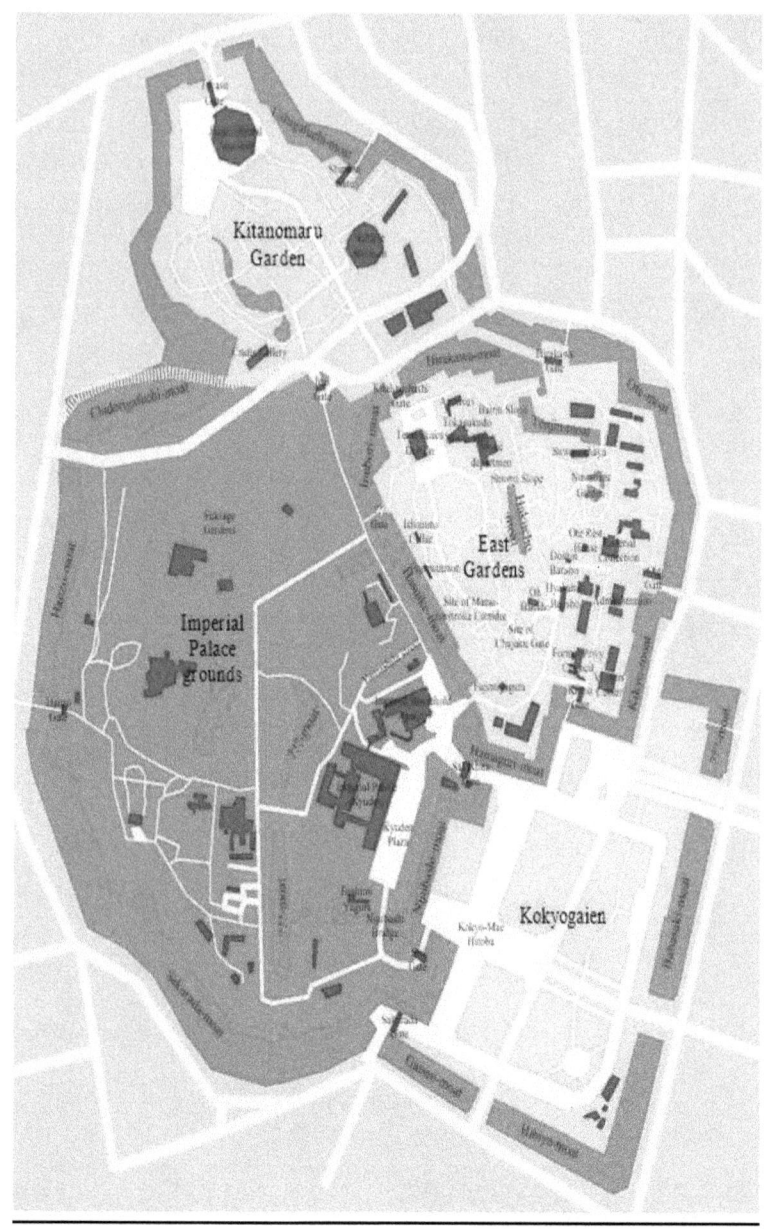

CHAPTER 39
In the Palace of the Japanese Emperor

During my stay in Tokyo, I often went for walks through the magnificent streets of the city – on my own, or accompanied by others. I enjoyed those walks best when the two young Germans – Rupert Enderle and Frank Diesch – went with me. They knew me and my interests so well that I could be sure they would not let me miss anything important. Mostly, they took me to the Ginza – the main street. It is very modern and wide with heavy traffic. What a colorful hustle and bustle of shawls and kimonos! It was amazing to see such color and diversity among Japanese clothing… the Japanese people dress with even more fantasy than Europeans at a folklore festival. What splendid fabrics you can see in the streets of Tokyo! Seldom a pattern is repeated, and every dress is different. During the New Year's festival, which lasts a full week, girls

Nonni in Japan

and women wear their most beautiful kimonos and belts. The belts are very broad and are tied in a voluminous bow on the back. The kimono shawl is worn on top. That's why it seems as if the Japanese women are wearing a small knapsack or a cushion on their backs.

I saw Mitsukoshi, the huge department store, which is bigger than the biggest stores in Berlin and excellently equipped with all goods thinkable. The walls are made of marble... moving stairs take people from one floor to the next... seven or eight elevators operate continuously, escorted by lovely Japanese girls.

It is enthralling how agile Japanese drivers and cyclists are! To see them turn and avoid a collision is nearly too spectacular to believe. Japanese taxis don't wait at a taxi stand until someone needs them; no, they drive through the whole city all day long, through all busy streets and past railway stations. If you want to take a taxi in Tokyo, you only have to stop on the pedestrian walk, and within half a minute an elegant car stops and invites you to get on. Many taxi drivers have a hired boy whose job it is to watch the pedestrians incessantly. Almost every car stops when he sees a pedestrian: the "co-pilot" waves with a smile to welcome his rider aboard.

In Tokyo City, an enormous amount of traffic flows through broad and modern streets; but in the suburbs, traffic winds around poles or glaring advertising arches, under colorful little paper trees and paper streamers and Japanese lanterns. Shops are not indoors like in Iceland or elsewhere; the central part of each shop is open on the street, with wooden merchandise displays installed in the back of the shop at a certain height, getting lower and lower out into the street, looking like a roof. The seller does not stand behind a counter, but instead sits toward the back of the shop on a mat. One feels more like being on a fairground than on a street. There are many people in colorful kimonos and shawls, and a lot of children and dogs.

Cute houses, signs in Japanese and Chinese characters, splendid colors everywhere, and extraordinarily beautiful kimonos on women and girls – all shape the life and activity in Japan. The residential areas are a few steps off the street, and in the most meticulous order. A little wooden door separates the small Japanese house from the rest of the world. Behind the threshold there is a small patch of a stone floor where you take off your shoes and walk in your socks or put on sandals which you will find at the entrance to every house. Inside the house are pretty rooms with soft floors made of mats. The walls consist only of paper-covered sliding lattice doors. You can hear in the whole house every word spoken in a room. In front of the house you only have to call *"Konnichiwa"* ("Hello") and the servant girl answers "*Hei*" ("Yes/Hello") and you can enter.

"In a Japanese house, you have to be aware of two things: rats and draughts," said a man who had travelled the world and once talked with Rupert Enderle and me about life in Tokyo. "You can enter a Japanese house from all sides because it consists completely of sliding doors, and therefore, draught cannot be avoided. Secondly: as long as I hear the rats gnawing in the house, I sleep calmly, for I know for sure that everything was in order. If it becomes silent in the house, however, an earthquake or a tidal wave can be expected, as the animals sense the change and move to safety. They are the best barometer. They sense every catastrophe much in advance! Hence the proverb: 'Rats leave a sinking ship.' There is even a legend that in China, two rat-folks had been in war with each other, and that afterwards eighty thousand rats bitten to death were counted on the battlefield!"

Nonni in Japan

Rupert Enderle, the enthusiastic young bookseller and editor, took me also to a street where you can find a long string of bookstores, one right next to the other. Beside many German books, you can find long rows of English, American, French books there, and even longer rows of Japanese literature. The Japanese read a lot: in the trams, on buses, trains – everywhere, you see people reading.

I found it interesting to see how many pictures of Holy Mary and of the Good Shepherd are displayed throughout the city. In one of the main streets is a huge YMCA building which also houses the only Japanese language school for foreigners in Tokyo. If desired, lectures from the Bible and Christian science and culture can be heard here as well.

My guides also allowed me to wander on my own if I desired. I had the opportunity to observe many more things alone than when

Nonni in Japan

I was in the company of others, but then, many things I saw I could not understand. For instance, not far from Jochi Daigaku University was a lake which seemed to me rather peculiar. Although this lake was not very large, it seemed deep. A man-made island arose from the water, with high and strange rocky walls which did not resemble formations made by nature, towering high into the air. Atop this island were big and small trees, behind which were buildings resembling palaces. One could only guess, however, because the splendor was concealed behind the shimmering leaves of the trees. This mysterious island was connected to the surrounding city by two mighty bridges.

The lake and its mysterious island aroused my curiosity. Furthermore, I noticed the men coming and going would bow very deeply as they passed along the bridges from the land to the island. There had to be something unusual and mysterious connected with that place! In the end, I asked a passer-by in English: "What kind of island is this? And who lives in the big buildings behind the trees?"

The man seemed to be astonished by my question. He answered in English: "This island has been built and fortified strongly, for in the palace behind the trees lives His Majesty the Emperor of Japan!"

So, this was the famous palace of the emperor – the unapproachable Tenno, the Japanese Mikado, whom the Japanese venerated almost like a god! Only then did I understand why passers-by turned towards the palace, took off their hats and made a deep bow. It is something completely different to see in person instead of just hearing about it!

I walked around the lake to get a better idea of it all, studying the two bridges leading across the water. I could not imagine the meaning. I asked another passer-by why such strong bridges had been built for that small island.

He answered: "The island is divided into two parts. The first bridge leads to the outer part of the island. You can get there without any difficulty. The second bridge leads to the inner part of the island and the Emperor's Palace. Very few people are allowed to go over that second bridge, for that is where the Emperor lives in his palace."

I pondered the view of that sacred site, never imagining that one day I might have the favor to enter this sanctuary.

After my walk that day, I returned to Jochi Daigaku University to see Director Heuvers and report what I had heard about the Imperial Palace and what I had seen on the fortified island. He asked: "Would you like an audience with the Emperor?"

I almost fell off the chair in astonishment. "Me? An audience with the Emperor of

Nonni in Japan

Japan? Are you serious? That would be an honor beyond compare! I could never expect such a favor. The Japanese Emperor is so highly venerated by his people that such a request would dishonor him! I could never dare ask for an audience with the Emperor of Japan!"

Director Heuvers downplayed my concerns. He said: "I believe that I shall succeed in getting an audience for you."

It was impossible for me to share his conviction, and I asked him quite seriously to give up the idea. Finally, he promised not to pursue the plan further. "But," he continued, "I shall show you into the Imperial Palace. You shall not have travelled to Japan in vain."

"I could better imagine that, and I would even accept it with great joy," I said.

"Very well," said University Director Heuvers. "Be prepared to go with me into the Imperial Palace one of these days." His confidence astonished me. Visiting such a place seemed to me, as a European, an impossible plan, especially as this is the home of the high Imperial Emperor. I did not have any special hopes.

But what happened? A few days later, into my room came the smiling Director Heuvers, holding a letter in his raised right hand.

"Are you ready to go into the Imperial Palace with me?" he asked.

"Certainly," I replied, "when the invitation or the permission has come."

Without answering, he placed the letter in front of me.

"What on earth have you brought me?" I asked, laughingly.

"A letter for you, from the Imperial Palace,"

"Incredible!"

"Not as incredible as you think. The Japanese are polite and friendly people."

He handed me the letter. I opened it. It was written in English: "Through the courtesy of the Imperial Household-Department, you are invited to the Imperial Palace…" Such astonishment! It was a double invitation: first a visit to the Imperial Palace, and second to a concert in one of the finest theaters of Tokyo (the "Gagaku"). Both invitations came from the Imperial Household minister. The letter was signed by "The Imperial Household-Department."

I was overcome! Director Heuvers had achieved everything which he had intended. I never thought it would be possible.

On the appointed day, I went with Director Heuvers to the Imperial Residence on the fortified island. On our way, he explained how our visit would go. A high Imperial official would receive us on our arrival (probably the same minister of the Imperial

Nonni in Japan

Household-Department who had written the letter). He would show us some of the extraordinarily splendid rooms of the palace. However, we could only see certain areas, as His Highness the Emperor resided in the palace, after all. That was quite okay with me.

Our car stopped at the entrance of the first bridge, where we were received by the Imperial guard. After Director Heuvers showed our identification papers, the soldiers gave way. Our car crossed the first bridge and soon reached the second. There, we had to show our papers again to enter the inner part of the island. The car drove a short stretch under high trees until we reached the entrance of the big palace.

Imperial officials helped us out of the car. An Imperial servant received us at the open gate of the Palace and helped us take off our coats and hats. Then, a very noble gentleman took us to a splendid reception

Nonni in Japan

room where we waited. Everything was so rich and splendid that we could not stop being amazed.

After a few minutes, the door opened and an extremely kind gentleman approached us, greeted us politely and invited us to follow him, going deeper and deeper into the indescribably magnificent Imperial Palace.

Since my friend spoke Japanese fluently, he did the share of the talking. I could not understand anything, of course. But that did not matter, because from then on there were so many wonderful things to be seen that the eyes had to do the main work, not the ears.

We walked through long corridors from one hall to the next. The splendor which we encountered cannot be described. I had seen beautiful Royal Palaces in various European countries, but nowhere did I encounter anything as rich and tasteful as here. All colors were coordinated,

Nonni in Japan

everything was calculated perfectly, with no tasteless exaggeration anywhere. We were in the Palace of the Emperor of a people whose art and culture are estimated in the whole world and who is regarded as one of the most intelligent people of the world.

In any case, I shall never forget that walk through the Imperial Palace of Tokyo.

When we had gone for a while through the halls of that fairy-tale palace, we reached a smaller room where our guide invited us to have a seat at a table with him. He wanted to fetch His Excellency, the Minister of the Imperial Household, so we thanked our guide, said goodbye, and sat down.

A short while later, the door opened, and the Minister of the Imperial Household came in. He greeted us politely and had a seat at the table. As far as I remember, he spoke English very well. But since my friend spoke Japanese fluently, as you know, both gentlemen switched to Japanese frequently.

Nonni in Japan

Sometimes they spoke in Japanese, sometimes in English. The minister was an extremely pleasant conversationalist. He knew how to render an interesting talk! Our pleasant chat lasted about three quarters of an hour, until we had to take leave.

We thanked the minister heartily for his invitation and said goodbye. He led us personally through the long corridors of the palace back to the entrance, where we got our car and rode back to Jochi Daigaku University.

Nonni in Japan

Addendum:

The 39th chapter is the end of the presentation of the journey around the world in the years 1936 – 1938 which Jón Svensson had personally prepared for print. His illness and death in the year 1944 prevented him from finishing this work himself. The remaining chapters, therefore, were compiled by his friend Fr. Hermann Krose, as closely as possible to the diary notes left by Jón Svensson. We present them now in a shorter form.

Chapter 40

Departure from Kobe in Japan

Nonni's departure from Tokyo took place on March 9, 1938. His next stop would be Nagoya the following day, where Nonni gave a long lecture to many Japanese listeners. From there he went to Kyoto, the old capital of Japan. Nonni found Kyoto quite impressive, with approximately 800,000 citizens and many interesting things to do. While there, he visited two Japanese kindergartens run by European missionaries and nuns, though educating the children in the Japanese way. Nonni saw boys between the ages of five and six performing gymnastics with an astounding perfection, and he witnessed girls of the same age dressed like shiny

Nonni in Japan

butterflies performing the most beautiful artistic dance.

Another memorable experience for Nonni in Kyoto was a visit with the illustrious Japanese senator Katutaro Inabata, a convert to Christianity who owned a wonderful 300-year-old park with canals, fountains and carp ponds. The senator held a banquet in Nonni's honor, with Nonni seated with the senator and his spouse. Approximately thirty professors, poets and scholars were in attendance. The guests rose one by one to introduce themselves, giving their names and profession. During the meal, several speeches were given in Nonni's honor, and at the end, many precious gifts were presented to him.

On March 13, Nonni travelled on to Osaka, a large seaport which is about two hours away from Kyoto by train. At that time, Osaka had approximately 2.5 million inhabitants. There, Nonni visited the Japanese school and institution "Tetukayama Gakuen" run by French missionaries. He gave two lectures in French.

In his diaries, Nonni says the following about this visit: "This Japanese school with 1,800 students is the best equipped institute I have ever seen. The whole establishment is admirable. The children are well-educated, well-dressed, well-behaved, and polite. The buildings and the playground are extraordinary. During my lecture, in front of an

Nonni in Japan

already huge audience, nearly one hundred more children entered this vast auditorium – but so quietly, so quickly, so modestly that I hardly took notice. The behavior and attention of all were exemplary. After the lecture, the school director gave me a Japanese mask as a present. It is the most precious gift I have received in Japan so far."

Nonni continues: "I was invited to give another speech in the theater of the newspaper *Asahi*. The big auditorium was completely full. I spoke about Iceland and its beautiful nature, describing adventures from my youth spent there. That evening, I was accompanied by my benevolent German friend from Jochi Daigaku University to give another speech for two thousand students in the huge national elementary school at Nara. One of the sights there is a big park with approximately 1,800 deer. When a trumpet is blown, they come running by the hundreds, even fighting with each other now and then! Toward us, they were very tame, especially towards me because I had brought them dry bread. Normally, the deer are only shown to princes and other distinguished strangers! In the evening, there were fireworks.

"Thus, it seems to me that Japan has adopted much of European culture, as it did with the Chinese culture before", says Nonni concluding this day in his diary. "But in both cases, Japan has converted these things to their own culture!"

Nonni in Japan

That evening, Nonni was driven back to Osaka by car, as he had more speaking engagements there the next day. From Osaka he went to Kobe, which would be his last stop in Japan before journeying home.

In Kobe, Nonni stayed with the Lutheran missionary Rev. S. O. Thorlakson, who was a fellow citizen and a friend of Nonni's. Kobe is one of the most important Japanese ports and has approximately 800,000 citizens. In Kobe, Nonni took part in three events which he called "extremely interesting." The first was in a kindergarten where six-year-old children performed theatrical plays. Even more skillful was the next performance in another kindergarten where Nonni took in approximately seven to eight plays. The third took place in a very posh hotel where storytellers performed fairy tales. Nonni had a turn speaking, and lectures were given about Nonni as well. When the program was over, he received many presents, and another great banquet was held. Guests included the Rev. Thorlakson and many Japanese priests. Nonni himself had several turns addressing the guests during the meal. The Japanese papers in Kobe, Tokyo and other big cities published very nice articles full of praise about Nonni and detailed his forthcoming departure. A reporter from an important Japanese newspaper had attended this last banquet and collected material for his report about the farewell party.

Nonni in Japan

On the day before his departure, Nonni visited the primary school "Azuma Chogaku." The 1,700 students performed beautiful dances in his honor. Later, another 2,300 students from the primary school "Schogaku" did the same. Even on that day, Nonni gave another lecture and a short speech on the radio.

The following day, March 18, 1938, Nonni's friends accompanied him to the huge Japanese steamer "Terukuni Maru" which was waiting in the harbor, and would carry him off on his departure home to Europe.

Chapter 41

From Kobe to Shanghai and Hong Kong

On the quay, where the "Terukuni Maru" was lying in anchor, about 2,500 Japanese children and adults had gathered to say good-bye to Nonni. He describes his first impressions after boarding the ship:

"The many little Japanese children whom I had met during my lectures had come to my steamer as a token of their gratitude, as if I had been the greatest benefactor of the nation. Their devotion was touching. They did not part from me until the boat left, and they waved good-bye for as long as I remained in sight. I sailed away with the happy

Nonni in Japan

feeling to have helped to reconcile West and East – Europe and Asia – and to proclaim peace on earth.

"Opposite me in the first class of the ship I met a young Japanese university student, Shoichi Washio, from Tokyo. He gave me a copy of the prominent Japanese paper 'Imperial University News' containing an article about Professor Ichikawa and my visit. The young man also showed me an Icelandic newspaper from Canada which had printed what I had written about Professor Ichikawa and his Icelandic lectures in Tokyo. The student was on his way to Oxford to study Icelandic. He seemed distinguished, polite and unpretentious."

Nonni continues, telling of three gentlemen he met and befriended on board: "During dinner, I met two Americans and one Australian. I was astonished that people seemed to know me at once and approached me without further ado. All told me their astonishment the farewell I received in Kobe, with so many children cheering. 'I have not seen anything like that in my life', said the Australian."

Nonni writes that the following morning, he took breakfast in his cabin, having requested Quaker Oats from the steward. Later, he reflects: "Many people have asked me about Iceland and my books, including six young journalists. I have met many different people already, including several Japanese women in beautifully embroidered silk dresses and a man in Japanese outfit - but with very dark skin,

Nonni in Japan

and a fez on his head. I asked him if he is Japanese. 'No', he said, 'I am from Manchukuo.'"

Next, Nonni details scenes along the ship's journey, such as this: "We are passing the Japanese port of Moji. The city sits in a wide bay, reminiscent of an amphitheater. It has approximately 100,000 citizens. About twenty huge merchant ships have anchored there and a swarm of smaller boats is either arriving or departing."

Nonni's diary describes other anecdotes. "Two distinguished elderly gentlemen are my neighbors. One is an American, the other one a true Englishman. Both have hearing problems; I often have to repeat the same until they understand what I said. They are very different. The American talks a lot and is very mild-mannered. The Englishman is extremely taciturn; he never says a word and hardly gives an answer. After dinner the steward asks me if I agree to have these two table companions as my neighbors at each seating. I say yes! Thus, we are tightly chained together for a few weeks.

"The Japanese children on board love me and shake hands with me when they see me. Among them are also the children of the Japanese diplomat Fuji, who is on board traveling to Prague. The children tell me that they heard my speech at the Seichin school in Tokyo. The adult passengers bring me Japanese newspapers in which they have found my pictures from the cities where I had been

Nonni in Japan

before my departure, and they give me the papers to keep. I am very popular on board!

"On the third day of my journey, a funny scene happened. My American table companion approached me as I was about to open my fountain pen, saying in haste: 'It does not work out that way, you will damage it.' Then he snatched the fountain pen from me, put it in his pocket and would not give it back to me, even though I asked him for it! After a while, he reached into his pocket and was most astonished to get two fountain pens of the same size – mine and his own. 'I thought you had my pen,' he said, rather embarrassed."

The diary then details his ship's landing in Shanghai: "The ship is now passing through an area of yellow mud flowing from the Yangtzekiang. We are going upriver slowly, stopping often and meeting many big and small boats. At the landing site, two professors await me: one from the Shanghai Aurora University, the other one from the famous observatory in Zi Kawai. The walk from the ship to the university was very interesting. Loudly singing Chinese workers carried my luggage and other goods from the boat to the shore. The large auditorium of the Aurora college is converted into a hospital for wounded workers. On our way, we met many Chinese men – smiling and merry and always busy. They wore long clothes, open in front. On arrival at the Aurora, I gave one lecture to the

Nonni in Japan

members of the French Mission, and afterwards, a second lecture for university students. Both lectures were received with great applause. During my speech for the students, there were newspaper reporters writing everything down, and photographers taking pictures of me.

"On our way back to the ship, there was a hustle of laughing, shouting and cheerfully chatting workers. In pairs they unloaded huge boxes and crates from the ship to the land."

Nonni's diary describes a rescue drill on ship the following day, whereby passengers practiced going to their assigned lifeboats which would be used in case of emergency. They also practiced strapping on life jackets, which Nonni called "an unpromising matter!"

The diary continues: "In the evening, I experienced a wonderful sunset on the ocean. The golden-red sun stands out prominently from the sky and slowly approaches the ocean, which surrounds our ship like a mirror. Eventually, the sun dives majestically into the immense sea. I watched with reverence as the sun reached the half-way point and everything turned purple and golden. Slowly, the glow faded, and then only a brilliant spark over the water could be seen. Finally, that went out, too, and the wonderful summer night began. Geographically, this was at the level of the Sahara."

Nonni in Japan

Nonni's diary is quite detailed as the ship eventually approaches Hong Kong. He describes the city as "situated in a fjord, framed on both sides by mighty heights and mountains. Huge houses are built on the hills looking like terraces. It seems as if one row of houses stands upon the other, up to the top of the mountain slopes. A very strange sight! The fjord is filled with a swarm of boats and ships, among them also big steamers. In total, I have counted around 120 ships and boats merely on one side of our ship! The Chinese junks which I can see here are often very old, their sails are torn, but they have always two: the big sail in front and the foresail at the back. I am astonished to see that the hardest work on the countless Chinese junks is not carried out by men, but by women wearing men's pants: rowing, steering, hoisting sails, etc. I ask a Japanese gentleman from Hong Kong about this. He says it was an old custom in China that Chinese men often hire little girls for such jobs. This gentleman is very knowledgeable. We go on to have an interesting conversation about celibacy, which he does not understand. He is astonished about my age and the strength which I still have."

Nonni disembarks and goes ashore with the American gentleman from the ship, all the while marveling at how hard the women seem to be working as the men appear to sit and direct them from their boats. The two men rent a car to sightsee. Nonni writes: "We drove to the top of the

Nonni in Japan

mountain, across the city, then downhill again. Wonderful roads hewn into the rock! The English do understand that well! Then we drove to a tremendously big hotel, just outside the city. Chinese boys are employed to open and close the doors there. They wear nice black uniforms with golden buttons and cute round caps which sit slightly crooked on their heads. Hong Kong is beautiful, the Chinese quarter, too."

Back on ship, a great number of new passengers have boarded in Hong Kong. Among them Nonni mentions a French Ursuline, a Mother Superior, who had received the request to go to Rome for a meeting of her order. When the ship reached Singapore, another Ursuline joined her – a Yugoslav nurse who would later render Nonni important service, when he fell ill. Nonni writes that he changed his seating arrangements in the dining room so that he ate from then on with the two nuns.

When Nonni boarded again after his excursion through Hong Kong, he writes of watching the agile Chinese women near the ship, with their black hair waving in the wind. Some women wore long braids, and all wore long pants and walked on bare feet. Nonni was struck by how nimbly they leapt between their boat and the shore.

Once sailing again, Nonni recalls how the Japanese passengers spent evenings singing. He writes: "It is a strange way of singing, completely different from the European way. The voice often rolls over, but not like the Tyrolean yodeling, nor is it a tremolo, but something quite peculiar instilling a special strong feeling and life to the songs. The little Japanese children in their colorful dresses remind me of multi-colored butterflies."

Chapter 42

Hong Kong to Singapore, Colombo, and Aden

Nonni describes the conditions as the ship sails along the coast of Indochina: "The weather is beautiful; the temperature, however, has risen to 30° Celsius. The sky is wonderful, and the sea is clear, blue and smooth like a mirror. Small clouds, far away on the horizon, shimmer like perfectly pure white wool." For a bit, Nonni had taken ill with what we may surmise was a nasty stomach or intestinal flu. He was fortunate to receive care from the nuns onboard that seemed to resolve the worst of it. Still, we cannot minimize the distress he felt, as he writes: "I am feeling better after taking some efficient medicine – a spoonful of medicinal mineral clay. Before that, I felt so weak and miserable that I began having the most somber thoughts. I imagined what would happen if I died onboard ship, and reasoned that, in this heat, my corpse would decompose quickly, so the poor captain would have to give the order to lower my diseased body into the

Nonni in Japan

Indian Ocean quietly. What an end that would be to my wonderful trip around the world! As I am feeling better now, though, I have regained courage and trust. But I have not yet recovered completely; I am still wearing thick winter clothes, despite 30°C temperatures, while other passengers are swimming in the pool on deck to cool off."

On this leg of the voyage, Nonni made the acquaintance of two Norwegian sailors on their way back to their home country. Their journey started with a three-year contract with a local shipping company, binding them to the service on the high seas while the company deducted money from their monthly salary to send to their families back home. Now that their three years were up, the shipping company granted them a free tourist class ticket to go home.

This is how Nonni describes the ship's approach to the quay of Singapore: "We can see Asians wearing all sorts of robes, with hats like lampshades; others with fezzes, or turbans of all kinds, or long hair tied up on their heads. Some headgear looks like colored rags bound around the hair. The people are half-naked, and their exposed skin is black, brown and tawny. Some wear skirts, and others wear short white trousers. The black-bearded Indian men show great control and self-discipline as they plunge into the water and jump back into their boats, nimble as fish. The Indian gentlemen look elegant in their light

Nonni in Japan

brown uniforms with saber and turban. The laborers loading and unloading goods wear snow-white jackets. Many workers wear only little trunks and a colorful turban, walking tall and swinging their arms with vigor. Most are bare-footed. They talk, shout, and make gestures as they work. The Moslems are quiet and recognizable by their fezzes."

The City of Singapore makes an idyllic image for Nonni: "Singapore is commonly known as the 'Garden City' because of its many trees and plants. Seen from the ship on the left is a towering island with trees and lawns and English fortifications. On the right is the city proper with about 300,000 inhabitants."

A Chinese gentleman, whose sister and her children were with Nonni's travel companions, offered Nonni and the two nuns a sightseeing tour of the city in his car. Nonni describes this as "a wonderful and very interesting excursion." He writes: "We met masses of Chinese and Siamese individuals: some men in long, shirt-like robes, while others were only covered with a waist band or trunks; the women all in smocks and wide pants. We saw beautiful shops along the streets. But the best of all came in the end: the enchanting Botanical Garden of Singapore – a mighty park with an endless number of rare, beautiful flowers and shrubs adorning wonderful paths. There were monkeys everywhere, too many to count! They roam free here, climbing high trees,

Nonni in Japan

sitting comfortably on the branches, eating bananas, nuts and whatever visitors throw at them. These sights are exotic!"

After the ship departed Singapore, the next city reached was Penang, an establishment of about 350,000 citizens. There could be seen a great number of boats, from small local vessels to impressive English and Dutch ships. The heat grew increasingly oppressive, and Nonni says he could not touch the railing without burning his hands. He soon ventured to swim in the pool on deck. Occasional rain showers brought cooler air.

On board, Nonni often talked with Shoichi Washio, a friend from Kobe and student of the Imperial University in Tokyo. He felt it a great honor to travel with 'Old Svensson' (as they say in Japan) and he granted permission for Nonni to write that personally in his diary.

Nonni also met two gentlemen from the Embassy of Manchukuo, bound for Rome; a Russian family; and a few Italian Salesian Brothers of Don Bosco. There were many Japanese fencing artists practicing on board as they sailed to Italy to showcase their skills there.

Nonni writes of this encounter with a young Japanese shipmate. "'Where do you come from?' the young man asked.

" 'From Iceland', I say.

Nonni in Japan

" 'So, you are a Dane?', asks the Japanese man.

" 'No', I say very decidedly, 'we have freed ourselves.'

"Then the Japanese man began reciting facts he knew about Iceland: the great millennium of the parliament, the foundation of its own shipping, of deep sea fishing, promotion of agriculture, production of tropical fruit with the help of warm springs. He also mentioned the beautiful language and literature, the sagas and Edda. I asked him where he had learnt all this.

" 'Oh', he said, 'I have read a lot'. That gave me quite a smile!"

As the ship sailed on, the next port of call was Colombo, the biggest city in Ceylon with more than a quarter million citizens. A longer stop was scheduled there. On shore, Nonni found it cost-effective to hire a car which could take him and the nuns to Mount Lavinia. En route, they passed crowded shops and churches, with people in white robes embroidered with gold and multiple colors. They also visited a splendid white church built by the Brothers of the Christian Teaching of John Baptist de la Salle.

From Colombo the ship traveled on to Aden. During that time, some Japanese passengers expressed interest in Nonni's company and invited him to dine with them. Nonni found it difficult to eat in the

Nonni in Japan

traditional Japanese manner, but his hosts made sure he had a regular chair along with knife, fork, and spoon instead of chopsticks. The banquet on board was described as impressive. Soft cushions were spread on the floor where most sat after taking off their shoes. There were multi-colored Japanese lanterns with meaningful inscriptions. Japanese gentlemen, ladies and children filled the room. The atmosphere was merry yet dignified.

Nonni writes of a moment onboard incident where he heard terrible sirens and strange calls between ships after going to bed. *What could that be*?, he wondered... *an attack by Chinese pirates*? It was nothing else but greeting another Japanese steamship returning from Europe.

Another day, Nonni partook in a Japanese pottery demonstration by the artist 'Rakuyaki' who was on his way to Europe. At a shared table, everyone had the chance to paint their own clay cup which was later fired in a kiln to permanently set the glaze. Participants kept their cups as their souvenirs.

Nonni writes more of the physical journey as the ship passes Cape Guardafui: "We are sailing along Somaliland, very close to the shore. It is a dry, burnt, mountainous country without any grass, only stones, debris, lighthouses, and a few shabby houses. On the ship, life is in full swing and everything possible is done to entertain us with movies and beautiful feasts. Cleanliness is

Nonni in Japan

exemplary on this ship. Generally, cleanliness is already important for the Japanese. However, even I am surprised to see that every night, everything (really – everything!) is washed and polished. When I get up early to walk around the ship, I see Japanese sailors polishing everything and waxing the linoleum floors. Even when I once left my cabin at 1 o'clock a.m. I found sailors sweeping and waxing! They strive day and night to keep the ship sparkling clean. Everything is dusted daily and gleams afterward."

Nonni continues his admiration of Japanese courtesy with this vignette: "One day three gentlemen in white uniforms come into my cabin saying, 'We beg your pardon. We are inspectors and would like to know how you are, and if you are satisfied with everything?'

" 'Yes, thank you', I answered, 'I have a single cabin for me, and a very good one at that.'

" 'But', said the officials, 'with five pieces of luggage in your cabin, you don't have enough space. The neighboring cabin is empty… we shall put it at your disposal until or unless anyone comes onboard and has need of that cabin.' So, now I have two big single cabins for me alone! Something like this has never happened to me before!"

Nonni in Japan

Chapter 43

Aden to the Red Sea and Suez to Port Said

Nonni follows the ship's voyage diligently: "Now we have reached Aden. It is Palm Sunday, and I go to church. The city lies in a bare crater landscape of a peninsula. The water supply comes from big reservoirs and gigantic cisterns. As I tour the surroundings by car, we are approached by long-necked camels and countless goats and donkeys. The landscape is all rock and boulders.

"When we arrived at the huge water tanks, our Arab guide says they had been installed by King Solomon. In any case, they look rather strange! The car takes us deep below the surface, through long corridors which are lit by electricity. The people we meet are all Arabs dressed in wide linen robes and wonderful turbans."

After Nonni is back onboard ship, he describes the scenic view of his surroundings. "The Arab coasts are peculiar, wide, gleaming-white stretches used for salt production. More and more ships are coming towards us in the Red Sea. It is – after all – the main waterway from Europe to Asia."

Next, the ship arrives at Suez, in middle of the night. Nonni nevertheless takes up his pen: "The passage through the canal is a difficult task for the captain. I

Nonni in Japan

go to the bridge of the steamer so that I can watch everything closely. At first, we sail through a few small lakes, where the canal banks are sandy. Gradually, the passage gets narrower. Now, the canal banks are of stone and are only about 40 to 50 meters apart, and about one meter high. Except for our ship, there is no more room on the narrow canal.

"A narrow road runs along each side of the canal, and behind that is the vast desert. On the left, I can see a little town with white houses in the far distance. In the desert, there are some ponds and small lakes, and small shrubs – then, nothing but emptiness. To the left is Africa, and to the right, Asia, with big heaps of sand and stones on both sides. On the African side, there are shrubs, but on the Asian side, hardly anything grows. The African side has cultivated fields, houses, roads in all directions, boats, and a big ferry. All the progress on the Egyptian side was made in the last 20 years by the British. What a huge difference between the view of both banks! But also, where there is no vegetation on the British side, improvement is in progress. Soon, palm trees, lawns and small farms will appear. Many passengers speak of taking a train from here to Cairo to see the pyramids before returning to catch the steamer again."

Nonni then tells this vignette: "Suddenly, our ship comes to a halt. What has happened? Our ship is

Nonni in Japan

20 meters from the left canal bank. But nevertheless, it is moored to the shore with very strong cable ropes, and we stop because very big ships come towards us and want to pass by."

After the ship started moving again, Nonni tells of crossing a huge green lake with a considerable number of islands, but not the slightest trace of vegetation. They continued in a northerly direction toward Ismailia where Viscount Ferdinand de Lesseps, developer of the Suez Canal, had settled until his death. Many ships passed: big and small, rowboats and sailboats, and English, Danish and Japanese ocean liners. When the Japanese steamer 'Hakone' approached from the opposite direction, passengers took up flags, balloons and colorful ribbons and exchanged enthusiastic shouts of "Banzai! Nippon Banzai!"

Nonni writes vividly of Port Said Harbor: "There is enormous activity here! A swarm of boats encircles our ship and people are climbing aboard: magicians and merchants. The Egyptians want me to buy all kinds of things. I don't succumb to anything. They repeat their offers in all possible languages. But that does not help them: I always answer in Icelandic, and they go away in despair!

"A 'flying bridge' made of twenty air-filled tubes allows them onto the ship. But the ship is also fastened at the bank. In town, there is an enormous statue of Lesseps. On the houses the flags of almost all nations are flying. The Japanese sun and the Turkish half-moon fly peacefully next to Egyptian, English, French, and Italian Flags.

Chapter 44

Port Said to Mediterranean and Atlantic

Nonni continues his narrative on through the last leg of the voyage. "During this final part of the journey home, plenty of entertainment is provided daily: movies, all sorts of performances, tea-sessions – and, at ports of call, excursions, such as are being prepared to Naples and Pompeii. Today, for example, a movie about Naples and another one on Japan are being shown in the dining-room.

"The nights now are rather cold. The temperature during the day was still 16°C, but that is still a contrast for the passengers of 'Terukuni Maru' who only a short while ago experienced the tropical heat on the Indian Ocean. As we passed Crete and Greece, a strong storm set in and so did the cold. My rheumatic pains grew considerably.

"On 18th April we reached Naples, where I hired a guide to accompany me to Pompeii. I was quite interested in The Neapolitan Museum's exhibition on the antique roads where slaves drew the carriages instead of horses. The view of Naples in the evening when the city was illuminated was a

Nonni in Japan

delight… the wonderful surroundings made an enchanting sight."

That night, the ship sailed along the Italian coast at high speed to reach Marseilles by early the next morning. This caused the ship to rock so forcefully that even 'the seaworthy Nonni' felt seasick! He describes docking in Marseilles the morning of April 20th.

"Many ships were anchored at the impressive pier. Among them there was a big French steamer which bore the curious inscription 'Asni', which is an Icelandic word. Everybody complained about the cold, but that lasted only for two days. In the harbor, the boat's cargo was rapidly but carefully unloaded by huge cranes. I disembarked to see a few friends from my time as a student in France, when I often went from Amiens to Marseilles."

That night, the ship sailed toward Gibraltar, where the weather warmed again. They docked at 7 o'clock the next morning. Nonni writes that Gibraltar looked a little like Hong Kong, with rows of houses built as if they on terraces. The stop there was short and only served for loading and unloading more cargo. Then, the 'Terukuni Maru' steamed on through the strait of Gibraltar out to the Atlantic Ocean.

This is now the last stretch of Nonni's globe-crossing journey. A crewmember approached him

Nonni in Japan

with the request to sign several sheets of carton board as souvenirs for the crew to have. He gladly obliged, writing greetings and short vignettes in German, English, French, Icelandic, Danish, and Japanese. The Japanese photographer on board asked to take Nonni's photograph, and he agreed.

As the ship passed through the Bay of Biscay, Nonni writes: "The ship is shaking a bit and some people are seasick. Everything on board is perfectly clean this morning, as always. In the saloons, there are fireplaces with glowing coals – in reality, these are only electric flames surrounded by bits of glowing glass. The English passengers especially like the sense of sitting by the fire and warming themselves."

On April 27th at 5 o'clock in the morning, the ship approached the steep English coast near Beachy Head, described by Nonni as "shimmering white limestone."

Nonni was particularly taken with the sight of the London Docks. He writes: "Never in my life have I seen such an overwhelming stage! The docks are said to be more than 20 miles long. The Thames is navigable for large ships from the coast up to London, as the river is still 245 meters wide. When the weather is clear the docks must offer a unique sight. Today, however, it is foggy, as is so often true here. All we can see are huge cranes, warehouses, and an infinite number of ships. The power, size and wealth of this metropolis overtakes the senses. Our ship will anchor at Victoria Dock, and then will begin the passport checks and other formalities."

With that, Nonni's journey around the world reached its conclusion.

In summary: On August 28,th 1936, Jon Svensson began his voyage from London-Southampton to North America aboard the "Berengaria". From March 4th, 1937, onward, he crossed the entire span of America. In San Francisco, he boarded the Japanese steamer "Chichibu Maru" which took him to Japan. On March 18th, 1937, he landed safely in Yokohama and was taken from there to Tokyo. In March of 1939, Nonni left Tokyo and returned to London on the 'Terukuni Maru' as just described above.

Chapter 45

Concluding Notes and Reflections

The 80-year-old Nonni spent almost a year in Tokyo observing and learning about Japanese life, keeping a very detailed diary. Strangely enough, Nonni did not reflect much on the religious life of the Japanese. One reason may be that he, as a European, was an outsider not able to fully know the heart of this people, since even purely external things were very difficult to understand. He confided several such thoughts to his diary from which we cite only the following notes:

- "One of my friends at Jochi Daigaku once took me with him to a big Buddha celebration in a huge building. At least 20,000 pious people were present. Lotus flowers and other souvenirs were distributed. Songs were sung by the whole congregation. Bells were rung and pipe music was played all the time. Lotus flowers were thrown into the air."

- "The Japanese are perhaps the most religious people on earth. Often, they remain in religious meditation for hours without moving and therefore are ideal for Christianity!"

- "We entered a Buddhist temple which was still new, extremely clean and fine… a wonderful, richly decorated hall. We had to take off our shoes, and then we could go further into the interior where the monks meditate and pray together. The prayer leader has an elevated place/seat, the others kneel on the floor. When a monk falls asleep, which is easily possible due to the great and enduring silence, he is beaten heavily on the

Nonni in Japan

back with a long stick! The monks never eat any meat or fish."

- " 'What is the aim towards which these monks are striving forward when entering the convent/monastery?' I asked a young monk. 'To honor Buddha and to imitate him by serving God and practicing virtues,' he replied."

- "One must tread softly and speak softly at Buddhist monasteries. At night, the monks sometimes camp on a hill overgrown with trees near the monastery, meditating God's grandeur, benevolence, and love."
- " 'Who do you pray to?' I asked a Buddhist who daily prayed with his children at certain hours.
" 'To God!' was the answer.

" 'And what are you asking God for?

" 'We thank him every evening and ask him to protect us during the night. And in the morning, we ask him to accept our thanks for the past night and to protect us during the day...'

So close to Christianity, I thought! If ever they become members in Christ's church and participate in its blessings, what great believers they will be!"

Nonni in Japan

The young German Rupert Enderle, who had gone to Japan two years before Nonni and who had stood faithfully at Nonni's side during his stay in Tokyo, commented on Nonni's notes with recollections of their visit to a Buddhist monastery:

> "We had gone by bus for ten minutes, passed an avenue, and reached a steep stairway with many steps, where many Oriental beggars were sitting up to the top, striking a gong monotonously. We climbed the steps slowly. When we reached the top, we went through a big gate and found ourselves standing in the middle of the courtyard on a hill covered with crooked-fingered pines. We were surrounded by temple next to temple, pagoda next to pagoda. From one temple came soft singing with heavy gong beats. Priests in white robes sat on the floor while a prayer leader struck the gong in measured time. Dragons appeared under high archways and flocks of pigeons fluttered around the strangely formed roof corners. Feeding them costs two Sen. They easily approached me, sat on my shoulders, and clung to my hips

Nonni in Japan

and fingers, picking hastily from my hands. Others fluttered around me, and a swarm descended on the bits of grain falling to the ground.

"The temple complex is wide and spacious, covered by a beautiful roof; women in kimonos stand in front of long bell ropes and are silent. The bell ropes are considered prayer cords and are embraced reverently. There is a light flickering in the darkness of the interior. We did not enter because we would have to have taken off our shoes despite the winter temperatures and the cold of the stone tiles. A mysterious Chinese writing on the wall speaks to those who visit. Dragon heads appear like ghosts from tomb stones, for respected people were buried there. 'You should come here to this Buddhist shrine on 14th October', said our companion. 'On that day, more than half a million people with lanterns will walk over the hill and through the temple.'"

The young Enderle also describes the Catholic Church in Japan:

"There are many Buddhist and Shinto temples in the city. Mostly

Nonni in Japan

they are built in a protected place or on top of a small hill. By comparison, the Catholic church in Omori is situated directly on a busy street. When I saw that small missionary church for the first time, it looked strange to me. Both towers are low and have truncated roofs. Going through the gate, you enter a room with shelves and shoe racks for uncountable "getas", straw sandals and straw slippers. There, the Japanese men and women take off their street getas (or, street shoes) and exchange them for the small straw slippers. Umbrellas and other items are deposited there. You reach the real entrance to the church by going past that foyer of sandals. People wearing European shoes don't have to take them off. The church is small, but beautifully arrayed and clean, and has colorful stained-glass windows.

"When going to church, all Japanese women carry a white veil which they put on their heads and shoulders. What a beautiful sight: the multicolored kimonos, the white stockings, the slippers, the white

Nonni in Japan

veils – yes, in church the Japanese women look like the saintly women whom we know from the Bible. So lovely to see the long rows of women with veils on their heads proceed to the communion rail! After a girl has clapped her hands, the whole row gets up, bending their knees together. The "Gloria" sung by the Japanese is a beautiful but peculiar song. There are about two hundred Christians in church. We kneel in the last row. Beside us, there is a kind of podium covered by a Japanese mat on which Japanese mothers kneel with their children on their backs. The mothers breastfeed their babies to keep them quiet, or else walk with noisy infants to the foyer of sandals, where there is a window into church and mothers congregate. Toddlers romp about on the mat there, tugging at their mother's clothes or making impromptu excursions through the whole church, where they must be fetched back by their mothers. The Japanese churchgoer does not feel disturbed by them, and the toddlers are seldom punished. However, if a child does become too restless, the mothers will get up and swing them

Nonni in Japan

onto their backs, securing them with a fabric belt. The children are used to this and stretch out their hands and feet cheerfully. The mother bends forward, wrapping the fabric several times around the back, around the feet and around her own body. Then she can stand upright. Finally, a shawl is wrapped around the child and her body, followed by another drape of fabric: and thus, the little troublemaker is warm and attached safely. The whole procedure is carried out in church. Churchgoers all remove their coats, putting them on the church pews, before going to Holy Communion."

Nonni knew that in Japan there were hardly more than two hundred thousand Christians among about eighty million non-Christians. But that fact could not hinder his belief that the seed of his great predecessor, Francis Xavier, is ever rising among the Japanese.

Nonni was content knowing that everywhere on earth there were people of good will. Knowing this,

Nonni in Japan

he returned home in March,1939, after his long travels. Then he began writing another book (this time, for the last time) to bear witness to his journey. He wrote up until the year 1944. It was that year that Nonni died "with a serene and satisfied expression and feeling as if he was in a cabin on an ocean liner", as his biography reports ("*Jón Svensson. Ein Lebensbild*", Freiburg 1949). He had reached his goal and thus became a messenger of peace, as was his heart's desire.

Nonni in Japan

ABOUT THE AUTHOR

This story "Nonni in Japan" was written by the famous Icelandic author of children's books and Jesuit Jón Sveinsson* (up to now the only Icelandic Jesuit). He was born on November 16, 1857, at the farmstead Möðruvellir in North Iceland. When he was a boy his nickname was "Nonni" and that is why the 12 books about his adventures and experiences are called the "Nonni books." During the twentieth century readers of all ages throughout the world devoured the stories of his adventures and the Nonni books became bestsellers—published in approximately 40 languages.

Before Jón Sveinsson became a writer he traveled throughout Europe giving many talks about his adventures in his fascinating Icelandic motherland – the country of ice and fire. Children and grown-ups filled large lecture halls and listened breathlessly to

Nonni in Japan

the charismatic Icelander. With his white beard and kind blue eyes the tall man himself was an impressive figure who caught everyone's attention. He loved children and they loved him in return. They even sent him letters begging to be taken along on his journeys. His readers could scarcely wait for his next book to appear.

May this book's trip through the United States, Canada, and other countries be as successful as Nonni's first visit to the "new world" in 1936 when Jón Sveinsson arrived in New York by steamship. This was the first stop of his trip around the world at the age 80 instead of taking 80 days as in Jules Verne's famous science fiction story!

On his North American trip, he was a guest of Fordham University for three months. He then traveled to Winnipeg where he visited his youngest brother Friðrik and other Icelandic immigrants to Canada from Akureyri that he knew before

Nonni in Japan

he left Iceland as a 12-year-old boy in the autumn of 1870. The last stop in North America was San Francisco where he had been invited to stay at the university. After two months Nonni continued his world trip and traveled across the Pacific Ocean on a Japanese steamship to visit Sophia University in Tokyo for a year. There he was the guest of Fr. Hermann Heuvers S.J., the second president of the university.

In 1938 Nonni returned to Europe via China, the Indian Ocean, the Red Sea, through the Suez Canal on to Gibraltar, and finally back to London. After resting from the long journey Jón Sveinsson started to write two very interesting and fascinating books in German about his trip around the world, namely "Nonni in Amerika," and "Nonni in Japan." He finished writing the first one but unfortunately could only complete 39 chapters of "Nonni in Japan" before his departure on his last trip—to heaven. His lifelong friend Hermann Krose added the chapters 40 – 44 after studying Nonni's detailed diaries and Herder published the books posthumously. Nonni died peacefully on October 16, 1944 at the age of 87 in Cologne, Germany, and was buried there in the Melaten Cemetery.

*The author's Icelandic name is "Jón Sveinsson" but he changed it to "Svensson" once he started writing his books in German. He feared that his German readers might mispronounce his surname. Thus his "nom de plume" has become "Svensson" except in Iceland.

Nonni in Japan

Nonni in Japan

After the sudden loss of his father a son recalls a trip they had planned to make together. A trip to his father's homeland of Iceland some fifty years after he had left. In his sorrow the son decides to set out upon the journey alone in order to honor his father's memory. To set out upon a pilgrimage to Iceland.

This true story features many photos. A unique combination of personal, philosophical, and spiritual reflections this book's sense of immediacy and wonder seeks to literally bring the reader along on the adventure, while its sense of reverence for the Icelandic culture, land, and people sets it apart from other tales of Iceland. This is Iceland as seen both through the mind and through the heart.

All Chaos To Order Publishing books are in easy to read large print. Please visit us at www.c2op.com

Nonni in Japan

Nonni and his younger brother Manni are Icelandic boys who live in the charming town of Akureyri which sits by the Eyjafjörður Fjord in northern Iceland. Nonni is curious about many things yet forgetful of his parents' warnings, while Manni is quite innocent and pure of heart and loyal toward Nonni.

Thinking he can lure the fish out of the sea with his magic flute playing Nonni, with trusting Manni at his side, sets out upon the Eyjafjörður Fjord in a small rowboat in order to try. Great adventures follow in this classic and true story of virtue and vocation.

Pacific Book Review's "Best Children's Book" of 2014! (Fully illustrated and in large print).

Nonni in Japan

Jon Svensson was born in Iceland and became its first Jesuit priest. After a career in teaching and ministry, he became one of the world's best loved authors by writing his series of "Nonni" books. For anyone else, such a life would seem full yet, even at age 80, he still held in his heart a boyhood dream to travel around the world and meet all of God's people. Here, for the first time in English, is the incredible true story that proves that life does not end, but really begins, at 80! "Nonni in America" features encounters with historical figures like Jules Verne, Thomas Cook, and James Garfield. It also has great descriptions of early air passenger flight, the great passenger steam ships, and the golden age of train travel. Through Svensson's fresh look at American exceptionalism, "Nonni in America" has much to offer to the reader of today.

www.ingramcontent.com/pod-product-compliance
Lightning Source LLC
Chambersburg PA
CBHW050115170426
43198CB00014B/2581